CW00530734

Jasta 18

The Red Noses

OSPREY
PUBLISHING

Jasta 18
The Red Noses

Greg VanWyngarden
Series editor Tony Holmes

Front Cover

On the morning of 12 August 1918, Ltn d R Kurt Monnington was flying high over southwest Germany looking for trouble. Along with other pilots of *Jagdstaffel* 18, he had flown far from the airfield at Montingen in search of British bombers. The squadron had been alerted that a large force of 'de Havillands' had been sighted by forward observation posts, apparently headed in the direction of Mannheim. As the Fokker D VIIs of *Jasta* 18 headed east to intercept them, the fighters were hard to miss. Each was marked with bright vermilion noses, touched off with white radiator shells. They also boasted brilliant red wings as well. The rest of their fuselages were pure white, and each was emblazoned with the distinctive unit insignia of a black raven, emblematic of commander Ltn d R August Raben. The 26-year-old Monnington had further identified his own machine with a sinister skull and crossbones emblem and sombre black outlining on the fuselage and tail section.

At about 12,000 ft over Schirmeck, the pilots of *Staffel* Raben sighted two formations of bombers, 11 machines in all. They were also pleased to spot other German fighters approaching. The DH 9s were from No 104 Sqn of the Independent Force of the RAF, a strategic bombing group recently formed on 6 June. The stubborn crews of the Independent Force had been engaged in a costly programme of long-range raids on industrial centres and railways within Germany. As the DH 9 observers sighted the fighters approaching, they swung their Lewis guns into position – they had encountered the red-winged Fokkers before.

The two formations were soon attacked by up to 23 German aircraft, and Flight Leader Capt J B Home-Hay led his bombers into a 'fighting spread', with both formations forming a semi-circle and flying large circuits. The *Jasta* airmen were not deterred and a fierce combat ensued. After 40 minutes, Home-Hay chose to abandon the primary target and bomb nearby Haguenau aerodrome. Upon discharging their bombs the DH 9s made a run for the lines and lost their defensive formation.

Recognising his opportunity, Monnington closed in on one of the bombers in the trailing group and opened up. The fuel tanks of DH 9 D2931 were hit and its pilot, 2Lt O F Meyer, was doused in petrol. Monnington watched as the British pilot struggled to land the crippled aircraft before it burst into flames. Meyer landed it intact on Bühl aerodrome, where he and observer Sgt Wallace were taken prisoner.

At about the same time Monnington's fellow *Jasta* 18 pilot Richard Schleichardt was forcing down another No 104 Sqn aeroplane. Kurt Monnington would eventually be credited with downing six bombers of the Independent Force, taking his final wartime tally to eight victories (*Cover artwork by Mark Postlethwaite*)

First published in Great Britain in 2011 by Osprey Publishing, Midland House, West Way, Botley, Oxford OX2 0PH, UK

44-20 23rd St, Suite 219, Long Island City, NY 11101, USA

E-mail; info@ospreypublishing.com

A CIP catalogue record for this book is available from the British Library

ISBN: 978 1 84908 335 5
E-book ISBN: 978 1 84908 336 2

Edited by Tony Holmes
Page design by Mark Holt
Cover Artwork by Mark Postlethwaite
Aircraft Profiles by Harry Dempsey
Index by Michael Forder
Originated by PDQ Digital Media Solutions, Suffolk, UK
Printed and bound in China through Bookbuilders

11 12 13 14 15   10 9 8 7 6 5 4 3 2 1

Osprey Publishing is supporting the Woodland Trust, the UK's leading woodland conservation charity by funding the dedication of trees.

www.ospreypublishing.com

CONTENTS

FIRST DAYS IN FLANDERS

Among the more than 80 German fighter squadrons of World War 1 known as *Jagdstaffeln* or *Jasta*, the unit designated as *Jasta* 18 had one of the most unusual histories. It served with distinction for more than two years on various sectors of the Western Front. However, after its first 16 months of existence the unit underwent a metamorphosis as it switched identities, personnel, aeroplanes and locations with another first-rate squadron, *Jasta* 15. This highly unusual swap occurred at the behest of Hptm Rudolf Berthold, the iron-willed *Jasta* 18 commander. Berthold left an indelible stamp on the history of the *Staffel*, and marked the aircraft of his command with a dark blue colour scheme and bright red noses.

Once Berthold accomplished this unprecedented switch of two *Staffeln*, the unit now known as *Jasta* 18 was a completely different group led by Ltn August Raben – another *Staffelführer* of impressive ability. Under Raben (whose name translates as 'ravens'), the *Jasta's esprit de corps* was expressed in the application of a brilliant vermilion and white colour scheme on its fighters, which were additionally emblazoned with a raven emblem as a unit insignia. Consequently, under both Berthold and Raben the fighters of *Jasta* 18 were identified – at least in part – by vivid red engine cowlings. The flamboyant appearance of these scarlet-nosed aeroplanes and the obvious skill of their pilots made quite an impact on Allied airmen. British and American aviators frequently mistook *Jasta* 18

The first commander of *Jasta* 18 was Karl Heino Grieffenhagen, seen on the left here with the more famous *Staffelführer* Manfred *Freiherr* von Richthofen. Grieffenhagen shares a newspaper with the 'Red Baron', who was in recovery from a head wound suffered on 6 July 1917. Von Richthofen holds his famous knobbed cane known as the *Geschwaderstock*. Grieffenhagen's *Jasta* would fly in the same Flanders skies as von Richthofen's unit in July and *Jagdstaffel* 18 would often be mistaken for the 'Flying Circus' by Allied airmen (*Arthur Rahn collection, National Museum of the USAF*)

(in both of its incarnations) for the 'Richthofen Circus' because the better publicised *Jasta* 11, led by the legendary 'Red Baron', also flew red-nosed fighters.

Royal Prussian *Jagdstaffel* 18 was officially formed on 30 October 1916 in accordance with the order *Kogenluft* Nr. 54427. The unit was formed at *Flieger Ersatz Abteilung* (FEA) 12, an aviation training and replacement unit located in Cottbus. The initial commander of the *Jasta* was Oberleutnant Karl Heino Grieffenhagen, a 27-year-old East Prussian. *Jasta* 18's first airfield would be located at Halluin, near Menin in Flanders in the German 4. *Armee* sector. Its opposition would be composed of the courageous and skilled airmen of Britain's Royal Flying Corps (RFC) and Royal Naval Air Service (RNAS).

The success of a fighter *Staffel* depended in no small part on its leader, and *Jasta* 18 was fortunate in this regard. Heino Grieffenhagen was born in Karklaugken on the first day of 1889, and he was commissioned in *Dragoner-Regiment* Nr 11 in November 1907. According to some accounts he was a pre-war pilot, and by 1916 he had seen service with *Feldflieger-Abteilung* (FFA) 12 (field aviation unit), FFA 45 and then *Kagohl* 1 (*Kampfgeschwader der Obersten Heeresleitung* 1 or fighting squadron of the Army High Command).

By August of that year Grieffenhagen was flying with the fighter detachment of FFA 32 known as *Kampfeinsitzer-Kommando* B (or *KEK* B), and he was still with that unit when it became the basis for the newly formed *Jasta* 1 on 22 August. In that distinguished *Staffel* he learnt from the example set by such noted Fokker Eindecker aces as Gustav Leffers and Kurt Wintgens. Although he would ultimately attain only two confirmed victories himself, Grieffenhagen was a capable commander who inspired respect and had a talent for instructing and leading his pilots to achieve their own successes.

It took several weeks for the full complement of Grieffenhagen's new *Staffel* to arrive, not to mention aircraft. Reporting in at the end of

The broad expanse of the airfield at Halluin was home to *Jasta* 18 from its first war flights until mid-June 1917. The sturdy wooden hangars were numbered one through four (left to right in this photograph) and feature prominently in many *Staffel* photos (*J Rief*)

October was the unit's first officer pilot, Ltn d R Paul Strähle. Arriving at the same time were three NCO airmen, Vzfws Heinz Josef Kammandel and Weichel and Uffz Flemming. November saw the arrival of Ltn d R Schreyeck, Ltn Fritz Kleindienst and Ltn d R Ernst-Ludwig Ritter und Edler von Loessl. Of this company, Strähle would prove by far the most successful, and also an able chronicler of the squadron's exploits.

Paul Strähle was born in Schorndorf on 20 May 1893, and he would survive the conflict as the leading *Jagdflieger* produced by his native kingdom of Württemberg. He came near to spending his war in Zeppelins instead of aeroplanes. On 1 October 1913, as a one-year volunteer, he joined *I. Kompanie Luftschiffer-Bataillon* Nr 4 at Mannheim. Strähle made a number of flights in Zeppelin Z VII, but upon the outbreak of war he was sent off to Brussels to help construct an airship shed as he had not completed some courses that were required for active Zeppelin service. Upon completion of the shed, Strähle was posted to *Luftschifferbataillon Stollwerk* and was disappointingly assigned to infantry duty in the Flanders trenches.

Having been promoted to leutnant der reserve on 4 June 1915, he finally managed a transfer to aviation and arrived at FEA 8 in Graudenz in November for training. His first assignment as a combat pilot was to *Artillerie-Flieger-Abteilung* 213 at Menin, and his operations with that artillery-spotting unit began there in mid-July 1916. Strähle's Pilot's Badge was authorised on 28 August, and in September he realised his dream of transferring to fighters when he was sent to FEA 7 in Cologne for further training. Subsequently posted to *Jasta* 18, he would soon fly over the same ground where he had huddled in trenches a year before.

Strähle lived until 1985, and his detailed diaries, flight logs and memories have proved a boon to researchers. He told historian Harry van Dorssen that he was happy to learn he would be flying against the British in Flanders. 'Da ist immer was los, da war Luftkampf Sport!' ('Something's happening there all the time, air fighting was sport

Ltn Walter von Bülow-Bothkamp poses with Fokker E II 25/15 during his early service with FFA 22. With a wealth of flying experience in a variety of machines and locales, von Bülow was the most veteran *Jagdflieger* of *Jasta* 18 in its initial days, and scored the unit's first victories

there!'). Like most German fighter pilots, he felt that there were more opportunities for victories, and honours, flying against the British than against the French due to the unrelenting offensive policies of the RFC (and its commander Maj Gen Hugh Trenchard).

The *Jasta* recorded a few orientation flights in December, which also saw the arrival of a 22-year-old nobleman of distinguished reputation and far-ranging service – Ltn Walter von Bülow-Bothkamp.

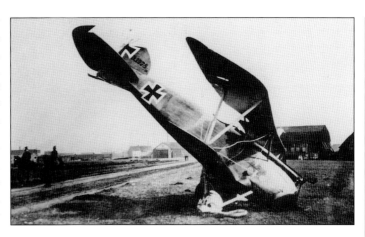

In its first months of combat *Jasta* 18 was equipped entirely with the Albatros D III, Germany's latest fighter, which played a vital role in the ascendancy of the *Jagdstaffeln* in early 1917. This example is 1978/16, which was damaged in a rough landing by Ltn d R Ernst Wiessner near Menin in the spring of 1917. Nonetheless, Wiessner would prove one of the unit's most able air fighters

Another promising newcomer was Ltn Gustav Nolte, a 21-year-old Hamburg native who joined the unit just before the end of the year. Equally noteworthy, a complement of Albatros D IIIs – the latest and most desired of German fighters – arrived to occupy the large wooden hangars at Halluin at the beginning of 1917. Although the new craft were eagerly test-flown when possible, the winter conditions delayed true combat missions, and there was little aerial activity by either side during the first weeks of 1917. Ltn von Bülow wrote home;

'Bad weather prevented us from clashing with the Englishmen, but they will perhaps be amazed by our new crates!'

The first 'war flight' of the *Jasta* occurred on 9 January, but terrible weather prevented much more activity until the 23rd, when von Bülow drew first blood for his *Staffel*.

Known throughout the air service as 'Jonny Bülow', Walter von Bülow-Bothkamp was born on 24 April 1894 at Birby near Eckenförde, in Holstein, and was the hereditary estate holder of Bothkamp, Holstein. Walter was the eldest of three aristocratic flying brothers. One of them, Konrad, would also serve in *Jasta* 18 as an adjutant. Walter graduated from *Gymnasium* (high school) in 1912, then took a tour of England and Switzerland, before studying law in Heidelberg.

After the war began he enlisted in the *Braunschweigisches Husaren-Regiment* Nr 17, which was one of three famous 'death's head' hussar regiments. Following service on the Western Front he won promotion to leutnant and managed a transfer to the *Fliegertruppe*, training at FEA 5 near Hannover. His first real combat assignment brought him to FFA 22 in the Champagne.

Flying Fokker and Pfalz monoplanes as well as twin-engined AEG G-types, von Bülow attained his first victory by downing a French Voisin on 10 October 1915, followed by a Farman the next day – earning him the Iron Cross 1st Class.

In 1916 von Bülow was chosen to fly in *Flieger-Abteilung* 300, which was part of the expeditionary *Pascha* I Corps assembled to support the Turkish offensive toward the Suez Canal. He arrived at Beersheba in Palestine at the end of April 1916 and continued to perform impressively in that exotic locale, even managing to achieve two more confirmed claims. Von Bülow was then posted back to the Western Front, and joining *Jasta* 18 on 7 December 1916.

FIRST VICTORIES

As noted, von Bülow finally had his opportunity to 'clash with the Englishmen' in a big way on 23 January in spite of the freezing temperatures and strong east wind. A flight of Sopwith 1¹/₂ Strutters from No 45 Sqn had departed on a photographic mission in the Ypres area at 1330 hrs (author's note – unless otherwise specified, times given in this volume are always reported using German time which was usually one hour ahead of Allied time). The primary purpose of the defensive *Jagdstaffeln* was to prevent Allied artillery spotting, bombing, or reconnaissance flights from succeeding in their missions.

Attacking the British two-seaters over Gheluvelt, von Bülow shot down the escorting Sopwith 1¹/₂ Strutter A1078, killing the crew of 2Lt J N Lyle and Bombardier A Harrison. The *Jagdflieger* did not have everything his own way, however, as he was forced to land with seven holes in his fuel tank (and was claimed as 'out of control' by another No 45 Sqn crew).

About two hours later he was again aloft, leading a flight of four Albatros D IIIs in an attack on an FE 8 pusher fighter from No 41 Sqn. Von Bülow's accurate gunfire claimed the life of 2Lt S F Cody, who nose-dived from 600 ft into the German lines near Boisinghe in FE 8 7613 (described as 'Vickers single-seater, Nr 7613' – a common error – in the weekly summary of air activities known as the *Nachrichtenblatt der Luftstreitkräfte*). These aircraft were confirmed as von Bülow's fifth and sixth victories. In the months to come *Jasta* 18 would continually encounter the 'Strutters' of No 45 Sqn, as well as the Nieuport scouts of No 1 Sqn and the FE 2d two-seaters of No 20 Sqn.

Two days later, Grieffenhagen proved a leader by example when he successfully claimed FE 2d A34 for his first confirmed *Luftsieg*. The big biplane from No 20 Sqn was forced to land near Roncq with a wounded pilot, and both crewmen became prisoners. On 26 January von Bülow and two comrades were on patrol on another frigid day. He wrote, 'Flying in severe cold at a great altitude really seeps into one's bones'. He again attacked a No 45 Sqn 1¹/₂ Strutter, the aircraft flying as escort to another machine on a photo mission to Halluin. Sopwith 1¹/₂ Strutter A1074 fell in flames in German territory, and Flt Sgt Webb and Cpl Fleming perished.

The string of *Staffel* victories was interrupted on 27 January when all Albatros D IIIs were grounded by order of the *Kommandierende General der Luftstreitkräfte* (or *Kogenluft*, the general in command of the air service). Structural failures of the lower wing were proving the Achilles' heel of the sesquiplane Albatros. *Jasta* 18's fighters were returned to *Armee-Flug-Park* 4 with damaged wings due to 'faulty workmanship', but by 7 February the *Staffel* had been re-equipped with new machines featuring reinforced lower wings. War flying resumed, and during the week of 11-17 February the *Jasta* recorded 36 patrols totaling 37.5 hours of flying time.

Early February also saw the posting in of Ltn Konrad von Bülow-Bothkamp (Walter's brother), Ltn Josef Flink and Ltn d R Ernst Wiessner. A native of Stuttgart, the 22-year-old Wiessner had started the war with *Feldartillerie-Regt* Nr 54. Having transferred to the *Fliegertruppe*

The FE 2d pushers of No 20 Sqn were repeatedly encountered by *Jasta* 18 in the first half of 1917. This machine is A9, allotted to No 20 Sqn in June 1916. On 20 October, when being flown by Lt H E Hartney with observer 2Lt W Jourdan, it was struck by ground fire and forced to land. On 14 February 1917 the same two crewmen were shot down by *Jasta* 18, although in a different machine

in April 1916, by the next January he was in *Flieger-Abteilung (A) 250*, but his stay there was brief.

On 14 February 1917 Paul Strähle and Uffz Flemming both racked up their first victories. FE 2d A1960 from No 20 Sqn had taken off on a photographic flight to the woods near Passchendaele, the aircraft being crewed by pilot Canadian Capt Harold Hartney and his countryman 2Lt Jourdan as gunner. Already credited with four victories, Hartney would later transfer to the American Air Service and command the 1st Pursuit Group. As related in his 1940 book *Up and At 'Em*, Hartney's aeroplane was escorted by FE 2d A15, flown by 2Lts Taylor and Myers. Many years later Hartney studied Floyd Gibbons' book *The Red Knight of Germany* and was convinced he had met the 'Red Baron' on this flight (von Richthofen did attain two victories on the 14th, but they were both BE 2s). It was not the last time that the aeroplanes of *Jagdstaffel* 18 would be mistaken for those of *Jasta* 11. Strähle left this account;

'A report of the air combat with the crashed English FE biplane on 14 February at 1700 hrs near Zuidschoote. The *Staffel* started in a formation of five machines at 1638 hrs. Towards 1700 hrs, the *Staffel*, coming from the south, met two FEs in the Bixschoote area at about 2600 metres. At first an attack by the *Staffelführer* and myself was not possible as the enemy machines turned steeply away. I therefore kept close to my *Staffelführer* and only attacked when I thought I could take one.

'My opponent made a tight spiral dive, during which I could only fire one burst before overshooting him due to my excessive speed. I now opened the throttle again and made a wide turn in order to assess the situation. With that I got onto the second FE, which I followed from over the lines towards Het Sas. At first he tried to escape from my attack in a snake-like fashion, but when that did not help, he pushed his nose down steeply and flew completely straight. During that dive I had him nicely in my sights, so that I could fire continuously. His dive became steeper and steeper so that although I was completely throttled back, I could not help

On 14 February 1917 Lt Harold E Hartney of No 20 Sqn was flying FE 2d A1960 (with 2Lt Jourdan as gunner) when he had the bad luck to run into *Jasta* 18. The aircraft was wrecked in a crash landing just inside Allied lines, and both Hartney and Jourdan were badly injured. Another crew from No 20 Sqn was also shot down, and the two FE 2ds were credited as the initial victories of Ltn d R Strähle and Uffz Flemming. Hartney is pictured here in American uniform after he later transferred to the USAS

overshooting him. In order to attack him again I made a short double turn, during which I cleared a stoppage in my right gun. By then I had completely lost sight of him, and since I was only 1200 metres up and the flak was shooting rather fiercely at me, I rejoined my formation from which I had wandered off a long distance.

'After landing I reported following the enemy machine to the Zuidschoote area, but did not claim him as I had not seen him crash. According to eyewitnesses of the lookout post *Antwerpen* in Bixschoote the machine descended vertically, turning over and over and crashing near Zuidschoote. The crash site was fired at by our artillery.'

Both Hartney and his observer Jourdan were badly injured in the wreck of their FE 2d, but were rescued by Australian troops and would recover in the same hospital. The other FE 2d crew also crashed behind Allied lines – Taylor survived his injuries but Myers was killed. Uffz Flemming was credited with one FE 2d (at Houthulst Wood) from this combat. It seems possible that Strähle claimed the machine of Taylor and Myers while Flemming accounted for Hartney and Jourdan. The latter RFC crew received confirmation for downing two of their attackers (one in flames), and Taylor and Myers were also credited with one Albatros in flames, although *Jasta* 18 had no known losses that day.

As temperatures slowly increased in March 1917, so did the intensity of aerial activity. Much of this was centred to the south of *Jasta* 18's operating area, in the Arras sector. There, the British First Army was preparing for a spring offensive and German forces were beginning to withdraw to their newly prepared defensive positions in the *Siegfriedstellung* (called the Hindenburg Line by the British). Still, there were opportunities for Grieffenhagen's pilots to make their mark.

At 1720 hrs on Sunday, 4 March, Josef Flink shot up a Nieuport two-seater at Elverdinghe for his all-important first victory. This was probably the machine from No 46 Sqn that returned with the wounded observer 2Lt Stewart, who later died.

11 March was a red-letter day for the *Staffel*, with four confirmed claims chalked up. At 1215 hrs two more of the hapless Sopwith 1½ Strutters from No 45 Sqn were destroyed near Zillebeke by Strähle and Flink, while Vzfw Kammandel entered the lists with a BE 2. Walter von Bülow added something new to the *Jasta* 18 game bag when he loaded his guns with incendiary ammunition and went after a British balloon. He wrote;

'Everything worked out very nicely. I saw the occupants jump out with parachutes during the first attack. But the "gas bubble" didn't want to catch fire, although I carried out several attacks. Finally, when I had fired off all my special ammunition, it burned. My two comrades did a splendid job keeping two English aircraft assigned to protect the balloon away from me. The other knocked down a third Englishman.'

Six days later, British infantry began to advance to occupy areas the Germans had abandoned in their retreat to the *Siegfriedstellung*. During the morning of that St Patrick's Day, a group of FE 2ds from No 20 Sqn were escorted over the lines by three Nieuports of No 1 Sqn. Paul Strähle related;

'When we arrived at Bailleul a squadron of four FEs and three Nieuports took off from that field and headed for Soully-Lille. Over Lille

This view of Ltn Walter von Bülow-Bothkamp is one of a series of informal portraits of many *Jasta* 18 pilots taken at a table in an indoor setting. The aristocratic von Bülow contributed to the impressive *Staffel* tally of four victories on 11 March when he flamed one of the British 9th Kite Balloon Section's gasbags (*Rahn collection, NMUSAF*)

I pretended to attack the FE that was nearest to the frontlines. I shot at a distance of 300-400 metres and forced him to disappear. I headed for the Nieuports and attacked one several times. After my fourth attack he disappeared for good. Then I approached another and made two attacks on him. I was quite sure that I had hit him because for a little while he kept going straight on (hanging downward) and eventually he kept leaning to one side. He finally went down with the tail swinging in the back.

'After I made sure that he was finished I followed the large squadron that was flying in from Polygon Wood to Menin. The second Nieuport I attacked lay completely destroyed north of Linselles. My second attack was successful. The pilot, an English *Unterleutnant,* was shot in the head. The aircraft had exploded while it was still in the air. The engine had to be dug out of the ground.'

Strähle's victim was 2Lt A J Gilson in Nieuport 17 A6617.

At 1310 hrs on that same day, Grieffenhagen destroyed a BE 2d from No 6 Sqn for his second victory. Ltn Flink narrowly missed becoming the first casualty for *Jasta* 18 when he was shot down near Reckem – his Albatros was destroyed but he escaped unscathed.

'BLOODY APRIL'

As March of 1917 drew to a close Grieffenhagen could be very proud of his *Jasta*, which had tallied 14 victories without a single loss. That would change, however, in the next month – a period famous in aviation lore as 'Bloody April'. It would prove to be the high-water mark for the *Jagdstaffeln,* as the ambitious pilots used their superior Albatros fighters to decimate the ranks of the RFC and RNAS. Chief among the successful *Jagdflieger* were the deadly pilots of von Richthofen's *Jasta* 11, whose

Ernst Wiessner successfully attacked a No 20 Sqn FE 2d on the 5th day of 'Bloody April' but apparently failed to receive confirmation. On the 29th of the month he was luckier when he downed his first confirmed opponent – yet another FE 2d from No 20 Sqn (*Michael Schmeelke*)

string of victories during the Arras campaign took them to legendary status. For *Jasta* 18 the month would bring both triumph and tragedy.

On the morning of 5 April the prevailing rainy weather cleared enough to bring out aircraft from both sides of the lines as the build-up to the Arras offensive gained momentum. The Albatros fighters of *Jasta* 18 became engaged in a running fight with their traditional foes from No 20 Sqn south of Ypres. Although still a relative novice, Ernst Wiessner showed his mettle by shooting up one of the big pushers at 1145 hrs. The crippled FE 2d forced-landed at Abeele, but it apparently was not confirmed as a victory for Wiessner.

Meanwhile, FE 2d A6385 – flown by Lt White with rookie gunner Pvt Allum – was also hard pressed. White managed to fire his rear Lewis whenever one of his attackers overshot him, and his fire struck Albatros D III 1942/16 in the engine.

Josef Flink, who had been shot down and escaped the previous month, was not so lucky this time. Strähle later wrote;

'Flink started at 1048 hrs and did not return. According to an Englishman captured two days later, Flink was captured uninjured due to a damaged engine. He landed at Neuve Eglise.'

On 7 April von Bülow joined with a few *Jasta* 28 pilots from Wasquehal in an attempt to prevent a formation of 20 Sqn FE 2ds from bombing Mouvaux airfield. Max Müller from Württemberg *Staffel* 28 attained his unit's first victory by downing one of the bombers. Another of the FE 2ds was shot up and force-landed south of Ploegsteert Wood with a dying gunner. This probably corresponds to a claim by von Bülow, which brought him into the ranks of the ten-victory *Kanonen* ('big guns'). Not one to rest on his laurels, von Bülow raised his tally to 11 with a Nieuport two-seater east of Ypres the very next day.

To the south, the much-anticipated French offensive of Gen Nivelle was launched. Known as the Second Battle of the Aisne, the assault collapsed after a promising start and forced the British to continue to apply unrelenting pressure against the Germans at Arras for weeks to come. *Jasta* 18 continued to patrol the skies over Ypres whenever the weather permitted until the fateful 24 April. In a familiar scenario, at 0700 hrs a No 45 Sqn 1½ Strutter crossed the lines on a photo sortie, escorted by six of the lumbering FE 2ds from No 20 Sqn. This time Grieffenhagen and his pilots joined with *Jasta* 8 in attacking the RFC formation west of Ledeghem. Once again von Bülow's lethal fire riddled one of the pushers and two *Jasta* 8 pilots scored during the scrap. There was no elation among the *Jasta* 18 airmen however, for they saw their respected *Staffelführer* shot down by the FE 2d gunners. Grieffenhagen was badly hit in his leg and lower jaw but landed behind the German lines. Yet worse still was witnessed by his horrified pilots.

The greatest fear of every aviator on either side was being trapped in a flaming aeroplane. After witnessing a British airman suffer just such a grisly fate, Fritz Kleindienst had remarked that, in such a case, he would leap from his Albatros. On 24 April, 'The machine of Ltn Kleindienst was set on fire in an air-fight by a British biplane', Strähle later recalled. 'Kleindienst jumped out just as he had said he would do some days earlier when we had talked about what we would do in such a case. We had no parachutes yet, so the jump meant certain death.'

With Grieffenhagen out of action, acting command of the *Staffel* was assigned to Walter von Bülow-Bothkamp. The headquarters of the *Lufistreitkräfte* later gave this report about von Bülow;

'His lively spirit, coupled with unshakeable calm, his lighthearted cheerfulness and his noble character made Bülow an especially valued comrade and an exemplary officer. He was no blind go-getter. He often liked to fly alone. On the other hand he had a masterful understanding of how to employ himself and his *Staffel* in a well thought out attack, and as soon as combat had broken out he fought his way through with an iron tenacity until success was attained.'

The fine weather of 29 April brought on yet another encounter with FE 2d bombers from No 20 Sqn. Under von Bülow's lead the *Jasta* took off from Halluin and knifed into the RFC formation at 1850 hrs west of Courtrai. This time Gustav Nolte claimed one of the FE 2ds east of Zillebeke for the first of his three victories. North of Courtrai, Wiessner also shot up a 'Fee' for his first fully confirmed success and Strähle took his tally to four with another. No 20 Sqn had two FE 2ds crews taken prisoner and the experienced duo of 2Lt Perry and 2AM Allum were both wounded and brought down in British territory, although they stated their pusher had been shot down by flak.

A SWORN BAND

By the end of April *Jasta* 18 had increased its record to 21 confirmed claims. The scoring continued unabated into May and the *Staffel* pilots no doubt remained in high spirits. 'Of course, we were all ambitious', Strähle recalled many years later. 'As in every unit, from time to time there appeared a "blue" one, but these disappeared fast as they simply did not get along with us. In *Jasta* 18 we were a sworn band'. Strähle also

Pilots of *Jasta* 18 are seen with their dogs as well as local poultry behind the officers' *Kasino* at Halluin. From left are Ltn Schreyeck, *Staffelführer* Grieffenhagen, Ltn d R Ernst Wiessner, Ltn von Bülow-Bothkamp (with bulldog) and Ltn Gustav Nolte (*Strähle*)

15

No 20 Sqn FE 2d A5149 was forced down on the *Jasta* 18 airfield at Halluin on 7 May by von Bülow, where it immediately attracted great attention. Note the partial cockade painted on the lower right wing panel, indicating that this was a replacement from an upper wing. This aircraft was repainted with German insignia and extensively flown by Strähle for filming from the air (*J Rief*)

stated that while everyone was eager for success, he never encountered leaders or comrades who sought unearned credit. That level of ambition was further evident on 3 May when Wiessner was credited with a No 41 Sqn FE 8 near Houthulst (2Lt Fraser was made a PoW). Wiessner continued his hot streak two days later with a No 20 Sqn FE 2d, while Flemming claimed another for his 2nd victory.

On 7 May acting *Staffelführer* von Bülow accomplished a singular feat that most fighter pilots only dreamt of. Not only did he force down an enemy aircraft intact behind his own lines, he brought it down on his

The No 20 Sqn crew of FE 2d A5149 – pilot Lt A W Martin (left) and gunner Pvt W C Blake – were happy to pose with their conqueror, Walter von Bülow, on the steps of the 'take-off hut' at Halluin. Their aircraft was the ace's 13th victory (*Strähle*)

own airfield! Fittingly, it was a machine from No 20 Sqn – FE 2d A5149, which was on a bombing mission and flown by Lt W Martin with Pvt Blake as gunner. Von Bülow's accurate guns shot through the compression chamber of one of the cylinder banks of the FE 2d's Rolls-Royce engine. It was 1200 hrs when the *Jasta* 18 groundcrew and pilots – Strähle among them – must have watched entranced as the big pusher (with a full bomb load still on board) settled gently down for a landing at Halluin.

The Germans had already experienced occasions when enemy airmen burned their aircraft on the ground after landing, so Strähle was prepared. Pistol in hand, he rushed toward the 'Fee' as it came to a stop and fired a shot in the air. Lt Martin clambered down and faced the nervous German. There was a moment of tension as the British pilot reached into the pocket of his leather flying coat – and handed Strähle his visiting card! The FE 2d's engine was repaired and the British national markings were overpainted with Iron Crosses. Strähle test-flew the two-seater and was badly shelled by German flak batteries, in spite of the new paint scheme. He later did a good deal of flying with it, having fitted it with a film camera so that operator Müschke could shoot motion pictures from the air.

On 10 May *Staffelführer* Grieffenhagen – now promoted to Rittmeister – returned to Halluin from the hospital, still displaying a bandaged jaw and limping with a cane. Although still unfit for immediate flying, he resumed leadership of the *Jasta*. This permitted von Bülow to leave. His impressive string of accomplishments had earned him a true command of his own, and he would be taking over

The photographer caught von Bülow (at right) in the midst of an animated conversation with Rittmeister Grieffenhagen at Halluin just as an aircraft overhead diverted his attention. This shot may also record the Rittmeister's return from the hospital stay caused by his wounds suffered on 24 April, as his bandaged jaw and cane indicate. Soon after Grieffenhagen's return on 10 May, von Bülow would leave to take over *Jasta* 36. D III 2227/16 was decorated in a similar manner to von Bülow's 1954/16, and this may have been another of his machines (*Strähle*)

Richard Runge joined the *Staffel* on 15 May 1917 and would achieve an impressive record which belied his spectacled and somewhat scholarly appearance (*Rahn collection, NMUSAF*)

Jasta 36. There, he would increase his victory tally to 28 and earn the *Pour le Mérite*. On 13 December he was given command of the prestigious *Jasta* 'Boelcke', but was killed in combat on 6 January 1918.

There were more changes in the air for *Jasta* 18 and indeed all the *Staffeln* on the British front. With the failure of the French offensive on the Aisne, the Allied high command decided to move the main theatre of operations to the British front in Flanders. Although the final objective of the new offensive was to force the German army from the coast of Belgium and turn its flank, this required that the hills known as the Messines-Wytschaete Ridge be taken first. This would bring the full weight of British forces into *Jasta* 18's sector. Furthermore, the RFC and RNAS units were gradually re-equipping with improved aeroplanes. Indeed, some RNAS fighter units were already flying the vaunted Sopwith Triplane, and the SE 5 (succeeded by the SE 5a) and the Sopwith Camel would appear in increasing quantities in the summer of 1917. From then on the struggle for air superiority would slowly shift in favour of the British.

Nonetheless, six days after von Bülow's capture of an FE 2d, Strähle used his new familiarity with the type's strength and weaknesses to defeat another of the No 20 Sqn biplanes on 13 May. The crew of A6645 crashed near Brandhoek, behind their own lines, and were unhurt. Strähle had his fifth victory. In the succeeding days *Jasta* 18's offensive potential would be bolstered by the arrival of Oblt Otto Hartmann and Ltn Richard Runge. Hartmann would eventually score seven victories as commander of *Jasta* 28. Runge already had one victory under his belt, and he was destined to become one of the leading lights of *Jasta* 18.

On 23 May, an offensive patrol of four No 20 Sqn FE 2ds had crossed into German-held territory when they were engaged by a flight of ten Albatros fighters. Once again, the pilots of *Jasta* 18 apparently joined forces with neighbouring *Jasta* 28. While Max Müller and Karl-Emil Schaefer of *Jasta* 28 each added to their scores in the combat, one *Jasta* 18 pilot would pay a heavy price. The ace FE 2d team of Capt F J H Thayre and his gunner Capt F R Cubbon MC reported;

'We crossed the line at 8500 ft at Armentiéres at 1505 hrs, and were immediately engaged by D-type Albatros Scouts. We immediately turned toward the lines, and when about half-a-mile from them fired a red flare and attacked. The fight, which lasted only about ten minutes, took place at close quarters. One hostile aircraft attacked us and came

across our front at a range of about 50 ft, and we fired about half a drum from each gun into him and he turned completely over and went down out of control and crashed in the vicinity of Zandvoorde.'

The 24-year-old nobleman Ernst-Ludwig Ritter und Edler von Loessl was severely wounded in this encounter and died the next day (he may also have been claimed by Lt Jenkin of No 1 Sqn).

In the evening of 24 May the *Staffel* entertained a visiting officer from a nearby anti-aircraft battery – perhaps in part to raise their spirits after the death of one of their own. The party in the officers' *Kasino* was also something of an apology. Earlier, harsh words had been exchanged with the flak officer because the *Jasta* pilots had been erroneously fired on by his AA guns. That evening was rainy and the pilots looked forward to a morning off due to the weather, so the festivities continued until 0400 hrs.

Before heading off to bed, Paul Strähle jokingly told their guest that he would shoot down his next opponent right 'into the arms' of the Flak officer. However, only three hours later Strähle was rudely awakened by his batman with the news that the skies had cleared and he had orders to do a patrol with another pilot. Soon the two *Jagdflieger* were flying north of Wervicq, no doubt struggling to clear their heads. At 0845 hrs

Seven sleek Albatros D III fighters of *Jasta* 18 are seen on Halluin aerodrome in the late spring/early summer of 1917, with 1956/16 at extreme right. Walter von Bülow's D III 1954/16 is next, with mechanics preparing the engine for testing. It displayed von Bülow's personal markings of dark outer wheel covers and a dark vertical stripe on the fuselage (*Strähle album*)

This photograph was taken within minutes of the one above, and it shows von Bülow's 1954/16 being run up in the flying position as two mechanics struggle to hold the tail down. It was standard practice to carry out lengthy engine runs on the ground, as well as full power tests in this attitude, to see if all lubrication and cooling systems were operating as they should. The next D III, 1970/16, was flown by Strähle (*Strähle album via A Imrie*)

they engaged a flight of Nieuports from No 1 Sqn at an altitude of
about 5200 metres. Strähle's fire hit the engine cowling, and pilot,
of Nieuport 23 A6678. In spite of his wound, Lt J R Anthony managed
to land his Nieuport – near the Flak officer of the previous evening!
After Strähle landed back at Halluin, he received a telephone call from
his erstwhile guest congratulating him on keeping his word.

The grievously injured Lt Anthony was treated at the Flak battery
and taken to hospital, but unfortunately he soon died. Anthony's
Nieuport was soon salvaged by the authorities for intelligence purposes,
but before it was taken away the rudder 'mysteriously' disappeared.
It turned up in the pilots' quarters in Halluin, and later could be seen
in Strähle's home in Schorndorf for many years. This souvenir was
displayed along with a deactivated bomb from FE 2d A5149.

One day later, on 26 May, Strähle continued his own private war
against No 1 Sqn when he removed another aircraft from its inventory

On 25 May Paul Strähle forced down
this No 1 Sqn Nieuport 23 A6678,
which landed near a flak battery
north of Wervicq. The pilot, Lt J R
Anthony, later died of his wounds.
Its Lewis gun would soon be
salvaged, and Strähle collected the
rudder, which was displayed in his
home in Schorndorf for many years
(*Strähle*)

Strähle strikes a pose in front of
Nieuport A6678, his seventh victory.
The damage to the cowling caused
by his accurate fire can be seen just
aft of the propeller (*Strähle*)

Strähle downed his third Nieuport from No 1 Sqn on 26 May 1917. He was cheated of yet another intact trophy when pilot 2Lt MacIntosh succeeded in setting fire to Nieuport 23 B1685 before he was taken prisoner. A disappointed Strähle can be seen at extreme left in a dark woollen stocking cap (*Strähle*)

Strähle's caption stated that this photograph shows fighters of *Jastas* 18 and 28 lined up on Halluin aerodrome circa May 1917. Machines marked with personal insignia of letters 'B', 'W' and 'R' may be noted – most are Albatros D IIIs (*Strähle*)

– his third Nieuport from this unit. At 0700 hrs the Württemberger, just six days past his 24th birthday, brought down Nieuport 23 B1685 west of Roubaix for his seventh confirmed triumph. Once again, his opponent landed his aircraft safely in German-occupied territory, and Strähle must have looked forward to having another prize to inspect. However, 2Lt R R MacIntosh managed to set his undamaged fighter on fire before his approaching captors could stop him, and Strähle was cheated of his trophy.

On 2 June 1917, the *Nachrichtenblatt* reported that, 'At the 4. *Armee*, very brisk activity by large reconnaissance and patrol squadrons'. The airmen of *Jasta* 18 responded, and achieved one of their last really successful days for some time. Ltn Gustav Nolte racked up a double, being credited with a Nieuport single-seater over Thorout (2Lt Waters from No 1 Sqn, PoW) and what was listed as a Sopwith Triplane over Coxyde to bring his total to three. Ltn Wiessner contributed an 'FE single-seater' at Zillebeke Lake at 1100 hrs for his fifth victory – but he would not enjoy his 'ace' status for long.

MOUNTING LOSSES

The resurgence of British air power would become painfully clear to the airmen of *Jasta* 18 as the month continued. Strähle's flight log records that at 0642 hrs on 4 June, he made a frontline patrol with Wiessner, Nolte, Flemming, Runge, Hptm Hartmann and recently-arrived Ltn Johannes Klein and Offz Stv Matthias Denecke. Strähle wrote, 'In an air fight Offz Stv Denecke was killed. His machine fell apart in the air and he came down at Houthem'. Many years later, he would recall, 'According to an entry in my war diary, it was a surprise attack by a Nieuport who came out of the sun with two others that mortally hit Denecke'. The 25-year-old Denecke probably fell to No 1 Sqn's Lt T F Hazell as his fourth of an eventual 43 victories. Hazell's combat report stated;

'0700 hrs. Saw five hostile aircraft east of Hollebeke and dived on them, firing half-a-drum into one of them – his left wing came off and he immediately went down. Decisive.'

The loss of Denecke's wing may certainly have been due to Hazell's fire, or possibly the infamous Albatros structural problems had claimed another victim.

The next day, Ltn d R Richard Runge was credited with a Sopwith at Dadizeele at 1130 hrs for his second *Luftsieg*. He apparently joined some of the formidable air fighters of *Jasta* 11 in decimating a formation of $1^1/2$ Strutters from No 45 Sqn. The bespectacled Runge had been born in Hamburg on 22 November 1890, and he would enjoy an impressive run of good fortune in the next three months.

On 6 June, the *Staffel* lost the services of the promising Oblt Otto Hartmann as he was transferred to the command of the neighbouring Württemberg *Jasta* 28. There he would bring his tally to seven before falling in action on 3 September.

On 7 June, the Battle of Messines opened with a shattering roar as 400 tons of ammonal laid in mines beneath the German lines on the ridge were detonated at 0410 hrs German time. As British infantry

Nine Albatros D III fighters of *Jasta* 18 are arranged on Halluin aerodrome. The photographer stood in the lookout tower on top of hangar 4 to take this dramatic shot (*Bruno Schmäling*)

advanced throughout the day, RFC two-seaters flew contact patrols to inform higher command of how far the assault was progressing. *Jasta* 18's role in the response to one such flight by the RE 8s from No 6 Sqn brought Ernst Wiessner his sixth, and last, victory.

'We made three front flights', Strähle's diary records. 'During the last (from 1642 hrs to 1805 hrs) Ltn Wiessner shot down a BE (sic), which fell vertically over the lines (Hollebeke). Thereafter, during an attack by FEs, Ltn Wiessner wanted to evade them by an almost vertical crash-dive, during which his lower wing broke off from the fuselage'.

According to Australian historian Russ Gannon, the ill fated RE 8 A4210 was attacked by four Albatros Scouts, whereupon four FE 2ds from No 20 Sqn entered the fight. The crack FE 2d team of Capts Thayre and Cubbon appear to have been responsible for the death of Wiessner, for they were credited with downing an Albatros Scout at Houthem. It was Cubbon's 21st victory and Thayre's 20th, but this highest scoring of all FE 2d crews would fall to a German flak shell only two days later.

On 16 June 1917, *Jasta* 18 left its familiar surroundings at Halluin and transferred to a new airfield, although it did not go far. The move was made just a few miles northeast to Marckebeeke aerodrome, and the pilots would house themselves in the elegant Castle de Bethune. However, Grieffenhagen and his men did not enjoy these spacious quarters for long. On 2 July they had to pack up and move to nearby Harlebeke, as Castle de Bethune was soon to be occupied by Manfred von Richthofen, the recently appointed leader of the new fighter wing

On 5 June Richard Runge destroyed his second confirmed adversary (but his first with *Jasta* 18) when he downed a Sopwith 1 1/2 Strutter from No 45 Sqn. This superb study of Runge in his Albatros D V 1060/17 was taken in the summer of 1917. The scout was marked with two dark fuselage bands aft of the cockpit, and it also had a dark nose and wheel covers too. Note the rack for flare cartridges and the tube for a signal pistol mounted near the cockpit, as well as the wing camouflage (*J Rief*)

The engine of D V 1060/17 is run up at an unknown location in the summer of 1917. This machine was previously identified as a *Jasta* 6 machine, but the photographs presented here prove it was flown at some stage by Richard Runge of *Jasta* 18 (*A E Ferko*)

A confident *Jasta* 18 group poses on the steps of the Castle de Bethune at Marckebeeke in this wonderful study taken in late June 1917. These men are, from left to right, in the bottom row, Ltn d Rs Strähle and Runge, Rittmeister Grieffenhagen (*Staffelführer*), unknown and a smiling Offz Stv Johannes Klein(?) seated on the top step – the man identified here as Klein is confusingly labelled as 'Ltn Weiss' in Strähle's captions, but there is no other record of such an officer in *Jasta* 18, and he clearly resembles Klein. In the top row, unknown officer in front of the stone lion, Ltn Nolte sitting astride the lion, unknown, Ltn Schober (sitting), unknown officer standing, and Vzfw Kammandel. Later, these same steps formed the backdrop for many photographs of von Richthofen and his men of *Jasta* 11 and JG I, as well as motion picture footage shot by Anthony Fokker (*Strähle*)

Jagdgeschwader I, and his favoured *Jasta* 11. The front steps of the castle would be the location of many famous photos of the Red Knight and his pilots.

Now that *Staffel* Grieffenhagen had settled in for what would be a lengthy stay in Harlebeke, the young pilots returned to their deadly business in the Flanders skies. Their strength was augmented by the arrival of 27-year-old Ltn Otto Schober on 13 June, Ltn d R Albrecht Weinschenk on 13 July and Oblt Ernst Wilhelm Turck, who came from *Jasta* 7, eight days later. By this time the unit's Albatros D IIIs were being augmented by examples of the new D V model which, sadly, was still plagued by structural problems.

On 11 July Richard Runge claimed a Nieuport over Becelaere for his third conquest. The next day 25-year-old Oblt Werner Jahns, who had been posted in four weeks before, gained his first victory by destroying a SPAD VII from No 19 Sqn at Quesnoy (Lt D W Weld was killed).

The *Jasta* lost one of its most experienced pilots on 28 July. This most likely occurred in a scrap with the formidable No 56 Sqn, just recently returned to France after a brief stint in England. The unit was already renowned for being one of the best fighter squadrons in the RFC, and its new SE 5s were excellent aeroplanes. In recalling 28 July, Strähle later commented;

'On this day I participated in three front flights. During another in which I did not take part, at about 2100 hrs, Ltn Nolte and Oblt Jahns

By July 1917 *Jasta* 18 had acquired several new Albatros D Vs. Here, Richard Runge poses with his groundcrew and his D V 1060/17 at Harlebeke. As noted, this Albatros was marked with dark-coloured wheel covers, spinner nose panel and two vertical fuselage bands (*J Rief*)

had an air-fight with several Sopwiths (sic) near Roulers. During this fight, Ltn Nolte, in a fast attack, overshot his opponent, who zoomed up behind him and shot him down. Nolte was hit in the neck, and during the spinning down the machine fell apart. Oblt Jahns' engine was hit and he made a forced landing. At about the same time Hptm Stenzel, of *Jasta* 8, also fell. He was hit, and his machine too came apart in the air. It was the danger of all Albatros D Vs which accounted for many pilots.'

Jasta 18 had been involved in a titanic evening melee that involved Camels from No 70 Sqn, SE 5s from No 56 Sqn and more Albatros fighters from *Jasta* 8. Gustav Nolte had apparently been targeted either by R Hoidge or G M Wilkinson of No 56 Sqn, both of whom claimed Albatros Scouts that broke up. SE 5s were still fairly new on the Front and were frequently misidentified as 'Sopwiths' by *Jasta* pilots, and they would continue to be for months to come.

The main British offensive in Flanders, the Third Battle of Ypres (also known as the Battle of Passchendaele), opened on 31 July 1917. As the air war accordingly intensified for the *Jasta* 18 pilots, the loss of veterans like Wiessner and Nolte drove home the realisation that their Albatros fighters no longer gave them a performance edge over their opponents. The latest British scouts such as the SE 5 and Camel were augmented by improved two-seaters like the formidable Bristol F 2B Fighter and the swift de Havilland DH 4 bomber.

Even more unsettling was the unwelcome news that Rittmeister Grieffenhagen was leaving the *Staffel*. The highly respected *Jastaführer* would fly his last patrol on 11 August. He then apparently moved on to the leadership of *Jastaschule* (fighter pilot school) II at Valenciennes. There, he would put his great experience to use as an instructor for the rest of the war.

Of course, the question now on the minds of Strähle, Runge, Jahns and the other pilots was who would now command the *Staffel*? Instead of promoting someone from within the unit, *Kogenluft* Ernst von Hoeppner chose to bring in an outsider to take over *Jasta* 18. When the pilots found out who their new leader was, they no doubt reacted with admiration, astonishment and, perhaps, some measure of trepidation.

Rudolf Berthold was coming to Flanders.

The 26-year-old Oblt Rudolf Berthold had earned his first victories as a Fokker Eindecker pilot in FFA 23 in 1916, and under his command *Jasta* 14 had been transformed into a crack fighter unit. The 'unbending Franconian' would bring the same demanding training methods to *Jasta* 18

THE BERTHOLD ERA

Rudolf Berthold was already a celebrated personality within the *Fliegertruppe* by the time he took over command of *Jagdstaffel* 18 in August 1917. Having flown at the front almost continually since the war's outbreak, he had already accumulated a host of medals, wounds and 11 confirmed victories. His reputation as an aggressive, indomitable and demanding taskmaster no doubt preceded him as well.

Born in Ditterswind in northern Bavaria on 24 March 1891, Berthold was the son of a Franconian forester. Having joined *Infanterie-Regiment Nr 20 'Graf Tauentzien'* in Wittenberg in 1910, he was seconded to the air service in 1913 and qualified as an observer in January 1914. After the outbreak of war he began flying as an observer in FFA 23. Berthold made many vital long-range reconnaissance flights during the advance to the Marne, and its aftermath, which earned him the Iron Cross 1st and 2nd Class by October 1914 – at the time he was the first to receive these awards in the entire *2. Armee* besides the commanding general, Karl von Bülow. The following month Berthold started his flying training, and by January 1915 was back at FFA 23 as a pilot.

His first aerial combats were experienced at the helm of twin-engined AEG 'battle planes', but disastrous results with these lumbering craft convinced him of the superior merits of the Fokker monoplanes. The Eindecker fighters of FFA 23 were grouped into a detachment designated *KEK* Vaux, and it was with this unit that Berthold attained his first victory on 2 February 1916. Now the combative Franconian was on his way, and by 16 April he had downed his fifth adversary. His scoring was interrupted nine days later when he crashed in a Pfalz E IV, suffering a concussion, skull fracture and a broken pelvis, right thigh and nose. Most believed his flying days were over, but Berthold said, 'I will fly again – even if I have to be carried to the aeroplane'.

Indeed, he returned in only four months, and on 24 August he shot down his sixth opponent, which brought him the Knight's Cross with Swords of the Royal Hohenzollern House Order (a high order that was generally known as 'the Hohenzollern'). During this period *KEK* Vaux was transformed into the *Jasta* 4, commanded by Berthold's good friend Hans-Joachim von Buddecke. In *Jasta* 4 Berthold raised his tally to eight, and received the *Pour le Mérite* on 10 October 1915.

Berthold gained a command of his own on 16 October when he was appointed *Staffelführer* of *Jasta* 14, then located at Bühl near Saarburg, in the sector of *Armee Abteilung 'A'*. It was with this unit that he perfected the training and leadership methods he would later apply in *Jasta* 18. On 12 January 1917, Berthold said of his pilots;

'They are thankful for the perfection of their training, even if this is ruthlessly strict, and I myself know no mercy as regards duty. Practice takes place in all kinds of weather, and we do banking, attacking, defending and – top priority – shooting. In the end, the results of firing practice are splendid! I am mercilessly strict.'

At the end of February *Jasta* 14 was transferred to Marchais in the 7. *Armee*. By 18 April, Berthold could write;

'In spite of the lack of aerial activity, I was able to bring down four aircraft by mid-April – one of these was an armoured French crate. My *Staffel* works very well, and the only thing missing is enough opponents. How totally different it is up in Flanders with the Englishmen! What *Jasta* 14 could perform up there!'

On 24 April Berthold's lower right shin was shot through during a bitter fight with a Caudron R 9. He commented ironically, 'Actually, it is rather striking that the first time I was wounded (on 10 February 1916) it was in my left hand, and them came the upper left thigh (broken) and now my right leg. Now only my right arm is missing a wound! But one really shouldn't think about this, otherwise one will turn into a coward'. He was back with the *Jasta* by May, but was unfit to fly for some time. Berthold's *Staffel,* though, destroyed nine French aeroplanes and two balloons from May through July. Then Berthold got the news he desired – he was heading to Flanders, but without his prized *Jasta.* On 12 August he was appointed to command *Jasta* 18, which by then was part of *Gruppe* Wytschaete of the 4. *Armee*. Berthold wrote;

'Now I must start from the beginning again. Up to now the enemy has had control of the air, so one needs good fighter pilots even more than infantry. With a heavy heart I say farewell to my men in *Jasta* 14 and travel alone once more to Flanders. My new *Staffel* first needs thorough flight training. I intend to use the entire month of August for test flying.

'Already the English offensive is beginning to fizzle out, just like the French operation on the Aisne.

'Finally my struggles for a better organisation of our fliers are showing some successes, since I recently gained the commander of the Flanders army as an ally. At my suggestion, four *Staffeln* will be combined into so-called *Jagdgruppen*, and these will be placed under the command of old, proven fighter pilots.'

On 16 August Berthold himself was placed in command of *Jagdgruppe* Wytschaete, composed of *Jagdstaffeln* 18, 24, 31 and 36. On 8 September *Jasta* 24 would be moved to the airfield complex at Harlebeke to share the field with *Jasta* 18.

Berthold did not actually 'travel alone' to Flanders. On 12 August, Strähle's diary recorded, 'Oblt Berthold, *Jasta* 14, takes over the *Staffel* and brings several pilots and mechanics with him'. It was customary to allow a new leader (especially one of Berthold's status and determination) to bring a few pilots from their old unit with them to their new command.

Arriving from *Jasta* 14 with Berthold were the lanky Ltn d R Josef Veltjens (Berthold's protégé), Vzfw Gerbig and Hermann Margot. Born in Erfurt on 2 April 1894, Otto Gerbig was a pre-war flier who already had four victories. Three *Jasta* 18 pilots would soon be leaving for *Jasta* 14 in trade, namely Vzfw Kammandel, Ltn d R Michael Paulin and Fritz Schabbel.

Of the pilots Berthold brought with him, Johann Joseph Hermann Mathias Veltjens would achieve the most. He himself preferred the spelling 'Josef', and was invariably called 'Seppl'. Born on 2 June 1894

When Berthold was transferred to command of *Jasta* 18 he succeeded in bringing along a few of his most valued comrades from *Jasta* 14. Foremost among these was Josef Veltjens, who like his mentor Berthold would win the *Pour le Mérite* and rise to the command of a *Jagdstaffel*. He is seen here in his red and blue Albatros D V of *Jasta* 18, marked with his insignia of a white winged 'Indian arrow' (*L Bronnenkant*)

The long-legged 'Seppl' Veltjens is pictured with a *Jasta* mascot named 'Bella'. Pets were a common part of *Staffel* life (*Rahn collection, NMUSAF*)

in Geldern, in the lower Rhineland, and growing up in Berlin, Veltjens became fascinated with automobiles and internal combustion engines at an early age.

Upon the outbreak of war in August 1914, he volunteered as an officer applicant in the reserve and was recruited into the elite *Königin Augusta Garde-Grenadier-Regiment* Nr 4. He was later attached to *Leib-Grenadier-Regiment* Nr 8, and his service on the Western Front earned him steady promotion. After several attempts Veltjens succeeded in transferring to the air service, and made his first training flight at Johannisthal on 5 December 1915. Posted as a pilot to FFA 23 on 10 May 1916, he chose the unit's shortest officer, Ltn Walter Gnamm, as his observer to compensate for his own weight (he stood 1.92 metres tall). Veltjens was commissioned a leutnant der reserve in January 1917.

It was in FFA 23 that Berthold first became impressed with Veltjens' skill as a pilot, and the two would remain close associates for the rest of the war. Berthold's evaluation of Veltjens read;

'He is fresh and imbued with a fiery and youthful fighting spirit, he is gifted with superior flying skills and promises to achieve outstanding results. Because of his fresh demeanour full of humour, he is very liked among his comrades.'

Veltjens followed Berthold to *Jasta* 14 in November 1916, where he scored five victories in seven weeks in the spring of 1917.

Berthold and his boys received a rude reception to the British Front on 14 August when DH 4s from No 55 Sqn attacked Harlebeke. RFC bomber squadrons were targeting communication centres and aerodromes in preparation for the second phase of the Ypres offensive. 'In the afternoon, towards 1830 hrs, four DHs dropped bombs on our aerodrome, destroying two machines and severely damaging several others (windows, clothing all gone)', wrote Strähle. '*Flieger-Abteilung* 8 next to us lost four machines, and all their others were severely damaged'. One of the casualties may have been Strähle's own Albatros D III 1976/16, for that aircraft disappears from his flight log. The next day he tried out a new D III, 1970/16, and reported, 'Machine climbs very well, good rpm but very tail heavy – not very pleasant'.

STRUGGLES OVER THE SALIENT

During the misty morning of 16 August, the British 5th Army launched the first phase of the Battle of Langemarck. Despite the low clouds and mist, the RFC squadrons were out in force. At 0805 hrs Strähle flew D III 1970/16 on the first patrol led by Berthold, along with Veltjens, Schober, Weinschenk, Turck and Klein;

Pilots of *Jasta* 18 enjoy a moment of relaxation in front of the officers' *Kasino* at Harlebeke. From left to right are Ltn d R Strähle, Ltn Otto Schober, unidentified, Oblt Werner Jahns and *Staffelführer* Berthold (with dog). In Strähle's album caption the labels of Schober and the 'unidentified' officer are transposed, but this author believes that Schober is indeed second from the left (*Strähle*)

'Oblt Berthold dived on REs. Klein and I attack. One SPAD attacked Klein and I chased him away. I was attacked by four to six Nieuports and got several hits in my machine. I then saw six to eight Triplanes above us, and I attacked a Sopwith flying over Langemarck. Both my guns failed to fire a round (levers broken), however, which was a great pity for otherwise he would have been a *sure goner.*

'In the morning a big British attack was launched. Apparently all is not well in the Ypres salient. In fierce counter attacks during the day the enemy was thrown back to the old lines, but only at Langemarck. To the west of it, he still held some territory.'

One of the Nieuports that attacked Strähle was probably flown by Capt Fullard of No 1 Sqn, who fired 30 rounds into an enemy aircraft attacking a SPAD at Poelcapelle for his 22nd victory.

In the coming weeks Berthold drove his pilots relentlessly as they contested control of the skies over the Ypres Salient. The *Staffelführer* insisted on strict flying discipline with tight formations – not only in the air, but on the ground! They were ordered to take off in the same vee formation in which they flew, a practice Strähle later recalled as 'madness'. Of his second flight on 16 August, Strähle wrote;

'Take-off – nearly all machines were airborne at the same moment, a wonderful sight but a bit dangerous. Over Westroosebeeke we were attacked by a patrol of six SPADs. Klein drove down a SPAD who had been too daring at Moorslede, where he landed safely. Oblt Berthold had several hits in his machine, From then on I always kept close to him.'

Johannes Klein's SPAD victim may have been Lt Shipwright of No 19 Sqn. It was Klein's first victory but hardly his last, for he would go on to rack up at least 15 more in *Jagdstaffeln* 18 and 15 and win the 'Hohenzollern' on 19 September 1918.

Opposed by some of the best RFC fighter squadrons, Berthold worked to have promising fliers posted in to strengthen his *Staffel.* One such individual was 26-year-old Oblt Harald Auffarth, who arrived in

Two Albatros D Vs of *Jasta* 18 show off their red noses, dark blue fuselages and tails in this photograph from a FA 33 album. The D V on the left belonged to Johannes Klein, who reportedly used a 'white belly band' as his emblem. In this case the broad band was only partially white and the top segment was in some other colour. Klein later flew a D V with a similar two-colour band, but reduced in width. At right is Harald Auffarth's D V marked with his comet insignia, which would later mark his Fokker D VII when he commanded *Jasta* 29. When Auffarth left *Jasta* 18 in October 1917, his D V stayed behind and was taken over by Turck. For some reason a rudder from a captured SPAD VII is propped up against the undercarriage of Auffarth's D V. On 22 August Auffarth's machine was shot up in a scrap with 'A' Flight from No 56 Sqn, but he was unharmed (*T Genth*)

Ltn Walter Dingel and his mechanics pose in front of his Albatros D V of *Jasta* 18. Dingel was one of Berthold's most trusted associates from their old days in FFA 23, and he followed Berthold to *Jasta* 18 on 4 September 1917. The Albatros displays the red nose and dark blue unit markings as instituted by Berthold. Dingel's personal emblem was a pale blue band around the fuselage (*J Rief*)

mid-August. Having flown in FFA 27 and FA (A) 266, Auffarth had no fighter experience as yet, but would quickly demonstrate his talents. In early September Berthold managed to have another one of his trusted comrades from *Jasta* 14, Ltn Walter Dingel, posted in. Dingel had first served with Berthold back in their FFA 23 days when he attained his first victory as a two-seater pilot (in July 1916), and had long been one of Berthold's most trusted comrades.

Such reinforcements were necessary in the wake of losses suffered by *Jasta* 18 as the Battle of Langemarck ended on 18 August. That morning Strähle was part of a six-man *Kette* (flight) along with Oblt Turck, with Veltjens and Klein flying in a lower patrol. His diary reported;

'Attacked five Sopwith Pups [sic] with red colouring. At a range of 150 metres my guns jammed. Gerbig attacked my opponent after me and shot him down – a pity that the attack was not made in close formation. Ltn Weinschenk was wounded in the leg (a flesh wound in the calf).'

Historian Russ Gannon has determined that the 'Sopwith Pups with red colouring' were in fact almost certainly SE 5s from No 56 Sqn's A Flight. The unit had recently indulged in painting their machines up in bright colours, and A Flight Commander Gerald Maxwell's SE 5 had a red nose, while his flight possibly sported red wheel hubs. It is likely Maxwell wounded Weinschenk, for he claimed what he called a 'black and white' Albatros out of control near Moorslede. Later that same day the reckless Berthold led the *Staffel's* third sortie. Strähle recounted;

'Vzfw Gerbig was shot down at 2045 hrs near Passchendaele on a frontline patrol with Oblt Berthold. Berthold's machine was shot up as always these days.'

In Gerbig, Berthold lost one of the capable veterans that he had brought with him from *Jasta* 14. Weinschenk left for the hospital and would not see further service with *Jasta* 18.

During this period the *Staffel* frequently flew in two simultaneous patrols as Berthold perfected his tactics and relentlessly trained his

Although not of the best quality, this rare photograph is important as it depicts Paul Strähle sitting in his Albatros D III of *Jasta* 18 at Harlebeke aerodrome. This is probably D III 1970/16 after it was initially painted in the 'Berthold colours' of dark blue fuselage and tail, although a red-painted nose is not easily discernible. Strähle's personal emblem of a white battle-axe is seen on the fuselage, and traces of previous insignia (including a differently placed axe?) can also be seen (*Strähle photo courtesy Bruno Schmäling*)

fliers – he usually led the upper *Kette* and Turck or Strähle (flying D III 1970/16) the lower one. Such methods paid off on 21 August when Berthold scored his 13th victory, and his first with *Jasta* 18. Strähle wrote;

'A SPAD two-seater [more likely a Bristol F 2B] passed above us and Berthold shot him down near Dixmude. Later we encountered Sopwiths, SPADs and Triplanes and an enemy patrol over the flooded area in the Ypres salient. Jahns passed very close in front of me at full speed while I was firing, and after landing he found that he had hits "from a Sopwith"!'

The same fog of war that led Strähle to accidentally fire on Jahns also makes Berthold's victim (elsewhere identified as a Martinsyde) impossible to identify.

The very next day a five-man patrol from *Jasta* 18 tangled a second time with the colourful SE 5s of No 56 Sqn's A Flight, again led by Maxwell. 'Over Bixschoote, five red Sopwith Pups [sic] attack us from above', wrote Strähle. 'I turn and open fire. Auffarth dives down and is shot about. In the melée I remained the highest. One Sopwith was "wrapped up" (attacked by several Albatros), however, it succeeded in escaping. I maintained top cover, and from time to time fired at one who got too cheeky by pulling up to my level. An Albatros patrol of ten machines was not energetic enough and five Triplanes flew over Jahns and myself. We finally lost track of Berthold and Schober, who went down too low. Schober chased a Pup. Berthold sustained hits from ground fire.'

In this hectic, yet bloodless, combat, it seems that Maxwell claimed Auffarth as 'out of control' and Jeffs and Sloley of A Flight also achieved victories.

The rivalry between the two opposing squadrons resumed on the evening of 25 August when Berthold led an eight-strong patrol in an attack on six SE 5s from No 56 Sqn, with six SPAD VIIs from No 23 Sqn also in the mix. The No 56 Sqn ace R T C Hoidge reported that, 'I fired about 75 rounds of Vickers at a blue enemy aircraft, which spun about 500 ft and glided steeply east, landing west of Roulers-Menin Road under control'. Strähle wrote that there were 'many inconclusive fights' and that 'Schober's machine had been hit several times'. It seems that Schober was Hoidge's opponent.

Hoidge's description of a 'blue' Albatros indicates that Berthold had already put his stamp on his new unit less than a fortnight after taking command. The *Staffelführer* decreed that all the aircraft of *Jasta* 18 were to display *Staffel* markings based on the uniform of his old infantry regiment Nr 20, with its dark blue tunic and red collar and cuffs. Thereafter, aeroplanes under Berthold's command (*Jasta* 18 and later 15) would be identified by dark blue fuselages and tail surfaces with red noses. In *Jasta* 18 the undersurfaces of the fuselages and tails were generally painted a pale sky blue to match the wing undersides. Often – but not always – the uppersurfaces of both wings were dark blue as well. *Jasta* 18/15 pilot Joachim von Ziegesar described the machines as 'Blue birds with red noses, that is, because all of the *Staffel's* machines were uniformly painted blue with red noses from the cowling to the cockpit'. A large emblem applied to the fuselage, usually in white, individually identified each pilot.

Fighter pilots have always been interested in assessing the opposition's aircraft. Having accumulated considerable time in an FE 2d, Strähle took the opportunity to fly a captured SPAD VII at the Moorseele airfield of FA 33 on 26 August. He reported, 'It is very good but a little unstable. The feeling of safety is greater than in the Albatros. Throttle operation a little strange. Landing and take-off good'.

On 25 August eight Albatros fighters from *Jasta* 18 scuffled once again with SE 5s from No 56 Sqn, and Otto Schober's machine was 'hit several times'. At some unknown date Schober overturned one of his D Vs during landing as seen here. His personal insignia was a five-pointed white star, here applied in an unusual attitude. The red and blue *Staffel* markings are obvious, as is the light blue underside of the fuselage (*J Rief*)

On 26 August Strähle test flew this SPAD VII B3504, based at the airfield of FA 33 at Moorseele. Capt Davidson of No 23 Sqn was flying it when he was forced down by flak and captured on 19 June (*J Rief*)

Berthold struggled tirelessly to turn the pilots of his *Jasta* into a disciplined and lethal fighting force. In the 1980s Strähle related his memories of Berthold's extreme methods to several historians. He recalled that Berthold did not know the meaning of compromise, but that 'he stood for restlos auskämpfen'. In other words, Berthold's byword was 'fighting to the very end'. Woe to any pilot who tried to give an excuse for breaking off a combat.

Strähle never forgot the three golden rules that Berthold unceasingly hammered into his pilots – 'Abbiegen kenne ich nicht, Motordefekte kenne ich nicht, Munition ausgegangen kenne ich nicht!' This idiomatic credo is difficult to translate precisely, but basically said, 'I don't accept turning away, I don't accept engine problems, I don't accept ammunition running out!' If the motor broke down, the pilot had to stay with the fight until he was down in the mud – then Berthold might believe him. Airmen whose guns jammed were supposed to stay in the dogfight, as the enemy could not know it, and were more afraid of someone who did not waste ammunition at long range. Furthermore, the pilots were supposed to laboriously check their own ammunition before a flight and not rely on the *Staffel* armourer. Berthold *might* accept a pilot's claim of gun stoppages or engine failure once or twice, but the third time he was out – and out of the air service, not just the *Jasta*. Unsurprisingly, Strähle also confided to one historian that Berthold was capable of a 'towering rage', during which no pilot dared test or disturb him.

By the time the rainy skies were slowly clearing in the first week o September, Berthold had succeeded in forging a disciplined and close-knit band of air fighters. September 1917 would be the most spectacular month in the history *of Jagdstaffel* 18. Paul Strähle left on two weeks' leave at the beginning of the month, and Oblt Werner Jahns was posted to the command of *Jasta* 28 on 4 September to replace the fallen Otto Hartmann. Nonetheless, *Jasta* 18 still had enough eager *Jagdflieger* to carry out the job at hand.

SEPTEMBER SUCCESSES

Appropriately, it was the *Staffelführer* himself who achieved the first combat triumph of the month. The sunny skies of 4 September brought out RFC reconnaissance aircraft in the morning. At 0825 hrs, Berthold shot down RE 8 B3411 of No 7 Sqn west of the British lines, Lt Wary and 2Lt Payne MC both being killed when their aircraft fell near Ypres. Less than nine hours later Berthold was leading two other *Jasta* 18 aircraft over St Jean, near Ypres, when he shot down his second RE 8 of the day, which also fell behind enemy lines. A4372 of No 9 Sqn came down with pilot 2Lt Moore wounded, but observer Lt Munroe was unhurt. It was the first double of Berthold's career.

The victory skein continued the next day as Klein jumped a Sopwith northeast of Tenbrielen at 0955 hrs for his second accredited claim. Later, Berthold defeated his third opponent in two days when he forced DH 4 A7530 from No 55 Sqn down behind German lines at 1528 hrs, Lt Neill and 2Lt Webster being lucky to survive as prisoners.

On 11 September two more of the big bombers were added to *Jasta* 18's game bag when Walter Dingel and Otto Schober destroyed two

Schober contributed to *Jasta* 18's impressive string of September victories on the 11th when he shot down DH 4 A7439 from No 57 Sqn west of Courtrai. Sgt S F Egdington and 2Lt E T H Hearn were both killed and their bomber was completely destroyed, as grimly illustrated in this view

One of Veltjens' mechanics in *Jasta* 18 was Johann Rief, and his album provided many superb photographs, including this wonderful view of Harlebeke airfield. Rief identified the pilot of each red and blue Albatros in his caption. At extreme left is Berthold's D III with his winged sword emblem on the sides and top of the fuselage. Next is the D V of Otto Schober, marked with a white five-pointed star. To the right of that is Veltjens' D V emblazoned with his white Indian arrow, then Auffarth's D V marked with his white comet insignia. At the extreme right is another Albatros D III flown by Oblt Turck, marked with vertical white-black-white bands. Berthold and Veltjens both achieved victories over RE 8s on 16 September (*J Rief*)

aircraft from No 57 Sqn. The DH 4s were engaged in a morning bomb raid to the Courtrai railway sidings when *Jasta* 18 struck. Schober claimed DH 4 A7439 for his first credited claim and Dingel probably accounted for A7582 for his second – all four RFC crewmen died. That same day Ltn Walther Kleffel joined the *Staffel* from *Jastaschule* I. A veteran of FA (A) 269, Kleffel was pleased to find old regimental comrade (from *Jäger-Regiment zu Pferd* Nr 6) Albrecht Weinschenk in his new *Jasta*.

Berthold was clearly in top form and the Ypres Salient remained a target-rich environment. On 15 September he was credited with what is sometimes recorded as a 'Sopwith' and elsewhere as a two-seater. This may actually have been another DH 4 from No 55 Sqn. The next day's work added four more claims to the *Staffel* total, bringing it near the half-century mark. At 1800 hrs, Berthold latched onto RE 8 A4693, flown by Lt Haslam and Cpl Linlay of No 6 Sqn. His unerring fire sent the two-seater down to a fatal crash west of Becelaere.

The *Staffelführer* was by no means done, for about 30 minutes later he attacked two more photographing RE 8s – this time from No 4 Sqn – over Zonnebeke, with Veltjens as his wingman. One of the observation machines crashed behind British lines with a dead pilot

and wounded observer. The other riddled RE 8 made it back with an injured pilot and a mortally wounded observer. These two were credited as Berthold's 18th and Veltjens' sixth victories. In addition, Auffarth and Turck both successfully claimed two-seaters for their first confirmed combat successes. 17 and 18 September brought bad weather to the Ypres Front, and the weary *Staffel* pilots had a welcome break from flying.

The British planned to resume their offensive at Ypres on the 20th, and the preceding day saw intense aerial combat all over the front. Berthold returned to his favoured hunting ground over Becelaere on the morning of the 19th, where another valiant RFC reconnaissance RE 8 crew served to bring his total to an impressive 20 confirmed claims. At 1530 hrs that afternoon, there was a large scrap between *Jasta* 18 and No 19 Sqn north of Moorslede. Only three days after his first victory, Oblt Auffarth chalked up his second by wounding Lt Patterson and forcing him to land his shot-up SPAD VII A8864. Lt Jones in SPAD VII B3528 was also shot up, while his fellow No 19 Sqn pilots claimed three Albatros Scouts out of control. *Jasta* 18 suffered no known losses, and its victory total had now passed 50.

The third main battle of the British offensive at Ypres was launched on the 20th with the objective of taking the Menin Road Ridge. The RFC performed prodigious acts of cooperation with the ground forces but suffered grievous losses in the process. It was also a day of great effort for *Jagdstaffel* 18, with Berthold claiming a SPAD east of Lake Zillebeke at 1130 hrs. Less than two hours later, Runge attained his fourth victory by destroying a Nieuport 27 fighter of No 1 Sqn near the same location. Veltjens attempted to add his own contribution to the day's carnage by claiming a two-seater west of Hooge, but was only credited with an aircraft *zur Landung gezwungen* (forced to land), which did not count as a full victory in the strict German system.

The feeding frenzy continued on the 21st when *Jasta* Berthold participated in a large-scale attack on SPAD VII from No 19 Sqn,

'Seppl' Veltjens put in a claim for a British two-seater downed on 20 September, but had to content himself with only a 'forced to land' credit. Here, his D V is mounted on a trestle for engine tests. The light blue painting of the fuselage undersurface and undercarriage may be noted

along with some SE 5s from No 60 Sqn, in the area around Dadizeele. Auffarth and Runge proved lethally proficient yet again, each claiming a single SPAD between 1940-1950 hrs. A third fell to Berthold's deadly fire at the same time. No 19 Sqn lost 2Lts Kirby, Inglis and McRae, all killed. Runge had made 'ace' by scoring on two consecutive days, while Auffarth had accounted for his first three opponents in one week.

The next day the Bristol Fighters of No 22 Sqn attacked ten Albatros scouts of *Jasta* 18 over Hollebeke. Berthold turned the tables on the Bristols, shooting down A7025 in flames at Lake Zillebeke and killing 2Lts Bell and Nowell. The Bristol flight leader reported that the lost crew had been shot down by a 'red' enemy aircraft, indicating how much of an impression the red noses of the Berthold *Staffel* made on their foes. That same day Veltjens claimed a Camel downed south of Ypres, but again had to content himself with a 'forced to land' credit only.

The *Jasta* was still flying some old Albatros D III machines, as well as D Vs and a few of the new Pfalz D III fighters. Although these were inferior to the latest generation of British aeroplanes, this seems to have been of little hindrance to Berthold and his well-trained band of hunters.

In the late afternoon of 25 September the *Jastaführer* edged closer to his quarter-century mark by ending the life of Lt Powers of No 19 Sqn, who fell at Gheluvelt in SPAD VII B3520. The cloudy weather of the 26th failed to prevent Berthold from racking up another victory. The

Berthold reached his 25th victory on 28 September. He commemorated that significant event by posing with his mechanics for this photograph, indicating he was still flying an Albatros D III at this time. The mounting of a floral wreath with the number of the victory total on an aircraft's nose was a custom that Berthold would continue once he took over JG II in 1918. The crack *Jagdflieger* in that formation would mark their own 'decade' victory tallies with similar displays and photographs (*J Rief*)

Staffel commander destroyed a Sopwith at Becelaere at 1200 hrs for his 24th victory – Lt Gould died in Camel B2358, one of four pilots lost from the same low-flying No 70 Sqn patrol flying in support of British infantry. Only 45 minutes before Berthold's success, Richard Runge brought his own score to six by downing another Camel (possibly from No 45 Sqn).

At 1230 hrs on Friday the 28th, Berthold led a well-coordinated assault on a flight of Bristol

At some time around October 1917, examples of the Pfalz D III began to arrive at *Jasta* 18, and one of these was acquired by *Staffelführer* Berthold. D III 4004/17 is seen here in full warpaint. The military serial number can still be discerned beneath the dark blue overpaint on the aft fuselage and at the base of the interplane strut, as well as on the factory finish silver-grey wheel covers. A distinctive version of Berthold's winged sword emblem appeared on the fuselage (*J Rief*)

Fighters from No 20 Sqn that were out on a photo mission. Auffarth (his fourth victory) and Veltjens (his seventh) both claimed English two-seaters in the area of Wervicq and Hollebeke, while Berthold added a 'Martinsyde' (sic). Bristol F 2B A7241 (crewed by 2Lts Tomlin and Noble) was shot down in flames while A7210 was also destroyed (Capt Campbell and Pvt Tester both killed in action). This day's triumphs enabled Berthold to reach and surpass the milestone of his 25th victory.

The tried and tested airmen of *Staffel* 18 closed out their most successful month of the war in a big way. On the morning of 30 September the *Jasta* came to the rescue of a German two-seater that was being harried by Sopwith Pups of No 66 Sqn over Gheluwe. The Pups, though agile, were by now outdated, and no match for Albatros fighters flown by pilots of the calibre of *Staffel* 18. *Staffelführer* Berthold sent 2Lt Warner down to a fiery death and Lt Boumphrey was forced down in a slow spin by Richard Runge to be taken prisoner. Capt Bayetto claimed to have sent an Albatros down smoking before he himself made a forced landing

Unfortunately the pilot of this *Jasta* 18 Albatros D III at Harlebeke airfield remains unidentified. The *Staffel* colour of dark blue was applied to the upper wing surfaces, fuselage, and tail and a black/white chevron motif was featured as a personal marking. The metal cowling panels were modified with additional louvres – a *Jasta* 18 hallmark. Oddly, the usual red painting of the nose section is not easily discernible. This may be due to a photographic effect, or perhaps it had not yet been fully actioned on this machine (*J Rief*)

in the damaged B2618 and was wounded. Lt Pritt MC similarly claimed an Albatros before he crashed safely in B2162. Auffarth and Veltjens also gained credit for Pups downed to bring the cumulative *Jasta* total to some 68 victories. For once Berthold was pleased with his men, the *Staffel* having averaged a victory a day in September without sustaining a single casualty.

OCTOBER 1917

The start of a new month was scarcely noticed by the combatants engaged in the fierce fighting on the sodden ground or in the air above it. On 2 October, Ltn d R Arthur Rahn, who would eventually score six victories, was posted in to the unit from *Jasta* 19. That same day a formation of five DH 4s from No 57 Sqn set out to bomb the German aerodrome at Abeele, adjacent to Harlebeke. By 0135 hrs the bombers had dropped their ordnance and were headed home when they were intercepted by Berthold and his eager band of hunters.

The *Jasta* 18 veterans were now experienced at breaking up a strong formation of bombers, but the crews of No 57 Sqn put up a stiff defence. Capt D S Hall, flying with observer 2Lt Hartigan in DH 4 A7568, described the attacking aircraft as 'V-strutted Albatros Scouts, dark camouflage, some with red cowlings, one with a gilt circular marking the shape of a chrysanthemum'. The dark blue colour scheme of *Jasta* 18 machines was easily taken for dark camouflage, while the pilot with the 'gilt circular marking' remains unidentified.

Hall's combat report provides evidence of the ferocity of the fighting that ranged from Roulers to Houthulst Forest. He wrote;

'When returning from bombing Abeele aerodrome in formation with four other DH 4s at 16,200 ft, enemy aircraft approached from the southwest, 500 ft above us. The DH 4s turned and attacked as the enemy commenced to dive. The enemy aircraft passed over the

On 2 October 1917, *Jasta* 18 pilots shot down three DH 4 bombers from No 57 Sqn. One of the victors was Richard Runge, who here strikes a pose with DH 4 A7583 as a mechanic tries out the Scarff ring and its twin Lewis Guns. The pilot, 2Lt C G Crane, was taken prisoner but observer 2Lt W L Inglis was killed (*J Rief*)

formation and turned quickly behind. The fight became very confused and DH 4 A7568 engaged about eight enemy aircraft at different times very closely.

'One enemy aircraft approached from the side. The DH 4 turned across its front and the enemy aircraft then came onto a parallel course, the observer firing about 90 rounds at about 60 yards. The main planes on one side of the Scout were seen to come together and it fell over sideways and dived vertically for about 8000 ft, flattened momentarily, and then again dived, and was last seen in a flat spin 10,000 ft below.

'Two enemy aircraft in succession passed across in front of the DH 4. One passed at about 600 yards and the pilot fired about 15 rounds. The Scout dived and smoke and a burst of flame were seen to come from the pilot's cockpit. One machine was later seen on fire on the ground by both the pilot and observer, and also the observer in another machine. The pilot obtained a shot at a second machine, crossing at 100 to 50 yards. About 30 rounds were fired and the enemy aircraft sideslipped, almost colliding with the DH 4, then stalled and fell over into a vertical dive. This machine was seen to go down for about 10,000 ft, stalling, sideslipping and diving vertically, in rotation, apparently completely out of control.

'A number of machines continued to attack and were engaged without decisive results being observed.'

Hall's report failed to record that No 57 Sqn lost three DH 4s as a result of the frenetic afternoon action. Richard Runge brought down A7583 intact near Roulers and was later photographed with his prize – the observer 2Lt Inglis had been killed but pilot 2Lt Crane was taken prisoner. 2Lt Halley and 1AM Barlow both died in A7451, as did 2Lts MacAndrew and Sidney in A7581. One of these fell to *Staffelführer* Berthold for his 28th tally and another was credited to newcomer Walther Kleffel for his first victory, falling at Roulers.

That same day, Kleffel was wounded in the calf – most likely he was flying one of the three Scouts credited to Hall as 'out of control' (the aircraft Hall saw burning on the ground may well have been one of the

Ltn Walther Kleffel shot down a DH 4 on 2 October for his sole victory of the war. Wounded in the calf that same day, he would later return to *Jasta* 18

This splendid *Jasta* 18 Albatros D V displayed the usual *Staffel* markings in red and dark blue. The pilot is unidentified, but he was apparently superstitious, marking his aircraft with an emblem of a four-leaf clover within a horseshoe. However, these lucky talismans failed to prevent the destruction of this machine, as seen on page 41 (*J Rief*)

In this photograph, which reveals more details of the horseshoe/clover D V, it can be seen that the uppersurfaces of the wings retained the factory finish of green and mauve camouflage, while the cross on the underside of the bottom wing was defined with a white border. The port horizontal stabiliser was covered in unpainted printed 'lozenge' fabric. The unknown pilot was one of those who transferred to *Jasta* 15 in March 1918, for the same marking shows up on an Albatros in that unit (*J Rief*)

DH 4s). However, Strähle's later diary entry (see below) contains a cryptic statement that Kleffel was wounded in the *evening*, while the DH 4 combats all occurred at 1330 hrs. His wound put Kleffel in the hospital for nearly a month, but he would return to fly in *Jasta* 18 again. In 1974 he wrote to historian Ludwig Zacharias, recalling the strenuous days he flew with Berthold, and the impact it had upon him;

'What should I tell you about *Jasta* 18 or 15? Both *Staffeln* were extremely successful. Berthold was a strange person, sometimes charming, other times not so nice. He didn't think particularly well of me. That's probably due to the fact that after returning to *Jasta* 18 after my wounding I often cracked up, because I always had to fly the highest – mostly over 6000 metres – without any of the aids that were later available for this altitude. Because of this I became extremely nervous due to the overexertion, which could of course be explained by the high altitude.'

On 5 October Paul Strähle returned from his leave and was presented with a new aircraft in the form of Albatros D V 4594/17, which he was destined to make more than 130 frontline flights over the next seven

Paul Strähle made his first ten-minute test flight in D V 4594/17 on the morning of 5 October 1917. It was eventually painted in *Jasta* 18 colours and marked with a personal symbol of a white battle-axe. Strähle took this machine to *Jasta* 57 when he assumed command of that unit in January 1918. Here, he runs up the engine on Wasquehal airfield in early 1918

Another group pose photographed in the *Kasino* garden at Harlebeke reveals the close-knit camaraderie among Berthold's dedicated pilots. From left to right are Schäfer, Runge, Turck, Dingel, Veltjens, Berthold, Auffarth, Rahn, Strähle and Schober. As Berthold himself stated, 'Old *Herr* Dingel' and 'Father' Turck were hardly high-scoring fighter aces, but made their own contribution to the unit's spirit and atmosphere by their 'decent character'. Turck would be entrusted with command of the *Jasta* after Berthold was wounded, and had difficulties filling the shoes of his predecessor (*Rahn Collection, NMUSAF*)

months. Perhaps a bit disappointed that he had missed out on the scoring spree of September, Strähle wrote;

'During my leave the *Staffel* has shot down thirty enemy machines. Berthold got his 28th. In the evening of 2 October, Ltn Kleffel was slightly wounded in the calf. Hptm Otto Hartmann, who used to be in the *Staffel* and flew in my flight, later CO of *Jasta* 28 and of the *Jagdgruppe*, was shot down in Flanders early in September, His successor, Oblt Jahns, also from our *Staffel*, was shot down at the end of the same month.'

A letter written by Berthold on 6 October reveals his pride in the accomplishments of his boys, as well as the toll that the previous month's supreme effort had taken on him;

'My *Jasta* 18 has become a crack unit. Already in September it brought its score to 32 victories [sic – Berthold may have counted Veltjens' two "forced to land" claims]. When it comes to aerial combat, there are now no more pilots who would have to take a back seat due to the lack of a victory. When it said in army orders a few days ago "The battle-tested *Jasta* 18", it showed that people generally see what an important factor this *Staffel* – which once stood so far in the background – has become in this horrible struggle in Flanders. This is not to my credit. I simply trained them and led them to the enemy. I showed them, my men, the attack. The attack itself, the vanquishing of the enemy – that is, the main thing – is the job of the crews. Its brilliant execution shows what an outstanding spirit lies hidden in the whole *Jasta*, in each individual!

'I have really settled in quickly with 18. Two good old friends stand faithfully by my side – "Seppl" Veltjens and old *Herr* Dingel. If "Seppl" stays alive, he'll achieve more wonderful successes. He's like a young hound. He still hasn't gotten the hang of it, though he has already

polished off a nice number of victories. He still lacks the eyesight and cold, calm calculation in difficult moments. But I will yet instill into him what's missing. Old *Herr* Dingel and "Father" [Ernst Wilhelm] Turck are loyal, never leave our *Jasta* in the lurch and, though they're not shooting down any more aircraft, they often help more by way of their decent character than by bringing down aeroplanes. They see to it that an impeccable tone, a respectable understanding and a suitable flying spirit remain alive in the *Jasta*. Every strenuous day of flying leaves me overly tired, so I can no longer concern myself so thoroughly with the external official and social life as I did before.

'Now for the fourth time the *Jasta* has mopped up a supposedly unassailable English bombing formation! Besides my opponent, two others were brought down. It's my 28th!! My mechanics are beaming. If we come back from a flight and no enemy is left lying in ruins, their faces are full of reproach. The fine fellows!

'Already in the last few days there have been signs of the infamous Flanders fog, which so much hinders flight activity.'

Low clouds, mist and rain were indeed so widespread in Flanders that very little flying was done by either side on 3 October. The terrible weather continued on the 4th, but the British ground offensive was resumed along a seven-mile front from the Menin Road to the Staden railway with the goals of taking Broodseinde and Poelcapelle on the infamous Passchendaele Ridge.

The weather improved just slightly on 5 October and the RFC deployed more reconnaissance and fighter aircraft. 'A wall of clouds in north Flanders, strong gusts of wind and rain', recounted Strähle in his dairy. 'Early this morning a lost British SE 5 with a 200 hp Hispano Suiza engine landed on our aerodrome. Great excitement!' The No 60 Sqn pilot who landed SE 5a B507 at Harlebeke was 2Lt J J Fitzgerald.

At the top of their game, the accomplished band of *Jasta* 18 hunters pose with their demanding, yet inspiring, commander in the *Kasino* garden in Harlebeke. This photograph was taken between 5 and 10 October, just after the unit had obtained 34 victories in one month. From left to right in the front row are Paul Strähle, 'Seppl' Veltjens, Rudolf Berthold, Harald Auffarth and Otto Schober. From left to right in the back row are Hugo Schäfer, Richard Runge, Ernst Wilhelm Turck, Walter Dingel and Arthur Rahn. The cumulative victory score of this group would eventually total 150 (*Rahn collection, NMUSAF*)

The *Jasta* 18 pilots thoroughly examined the pristine example of the superb fighter they had often encountered. Among the fascinated onlookers was newly arrived Ltn d R Hugo Schäfer, who would routinely fly a D V decorated with a menacing snake – eventually he achieved 12 victories in *Jasta* 15.

BERTHOLD WOUNDED – AGAIN

The heady days of triumph under Berthold's leadership came unexpectedly and abruptly to an end on 10 October. That afternoon the usual rains lifted enough for fighter patrols to take off on both sides of no-man's land. At about 1800 hrs, the pilots of *Jastas* 18 and 26 became embroiled in a massive scrap with A Flight of No 56 Sqn and Bristol Fighters from No 22 Sqn near Ypres. 'Dogfights with several formations of SE 5s, DH 4s (sic) and Triplanes', wrote Strähle, who mistook the Bristols for DH 4s. 'Oblt Berthold was severely wounded in the right arm (bone shattered). Ltn Schober was hit in the radiator and forced to land at Heule. Other formations of Albatros [*Jasta* 26] joined the fight. Two British machines were shot down by them, one of these disintegrating in the air. Oblt Berthold landed safely at our airfield in spite of half-severed ailerons and heavy bleeding from his wound'.

Among the *Jasta* 26 pilots in the fight was Ltn d R Xaver Dannhuber, who gained his eighth victory by shooting apart the SE 5a that Strähle saw break up (Lt Wilkinson of No 56 Sqn, lost in SE 5a B23). The No 22 Sqn crew of Lt Meggitt and AM 'Arch' Whitehouse may have claimed Schober (Whitehouse later became a famous writer of aviation fiction and history). It is likely that No 56 Sqn ace and *Jasta* 18 nemesis Gerald Maxwell, in SE 5a B502, was responsible for Berthold's terrible wound. Maxwell's combat report stated;

'At about 1700 hrs saw and attacked about 12 enemy Scouts east of Ypres. Dived on the tails of several enemy aircraft, firing a large number of rounds. I got on to one enemy aircraft's tail and fired a drum of Lewis and about 100 rounds of Vickers at very close range. Enemy aircraft went down very steeply and I lost sight of him. At 1710 hrs I saw a machine go

On 5 October Berthold's pilots got their first close-up look at a dangerous opponent when 2Lt J J Fitzgerald of No 60 Sqn landed his SE 5a B507 at Harlebeke due to engine failure. This machine had been flown by Lt Barlow of No 56 Sqn for seven victories before it went to No 60 Sqn on 10 September, and it is possible the *Jasta* 18 pilots had encountered this very machine in the air. It had also been flown by 2Lt Chidlaw-Roberts of No 60 Sqn when he was attacked by Werner Voss just prior to the latter's fatal combat on 23 September (*J Rief*)

down in pieces over Gheluvelt. Whether an enemy aircraft or one of our own machines I do not know [this was Wilkinson's SE 5a].'

With grim determination, Berthold somehow managed to land his crippled fighter at Harlebeke without the use of his right arm and was lifted from the aircraft in a semi-conscious condition. Berthold's premonition from the previous April (that his right arm was his only untouched limb, and therefore due for injury) had proved true. His right humerus was shattered beyond the treatment a field hospital could offer. Someone in the *Staffel* recalled that Berthold's sister was a nurse who worked as the matron of the *Viktoria-Lazarett* (Victoria Military Hospital) in Berlin. The *Jasta* sent a cable there;

'Would the acceptance of the seriously wounded Oblt Berthold be possible at the end of this week? Sister Franziska should be informed!'

In a few days a hospital train brought Berthold to Berlin, where he would spend four months in recuperation. He was spared amputation of his arm only through skilled surgery, although he would never regain full use of it.

Six days after Berthold's wounding, the *Gruppenführer der Flieger* for *Gruppe* Wytschaete of the 4. *Armee* submitted the following evaluation of his military performance;

'Oberleutnant Berthold has belonged to *Gruppe* Wytschaete since the middle of August, as commander of *Jagdstaffel* 18 and at the same time *Jagdgruppe* Wytschaete.

'It is primarily due to him that supremacy of the air has been achieved in the *Gruppe* since the end of August. He took over *Jagdstaffel* 18 on the most difficult spot on the battle front, which in a short time was able to yield accomplishments that are only possible under a leader who shows an extraordinary offensive spirit, daring and bravery, who through his personality alone can inspire his subordinates to extraordinary deeds. 37 enemy aeroplanes is the bag of *Jagdstaffel* 18 in the short period of its activity, 16 of them falling to the commander himself.

'His example also carried over to *Jagdgruppe* Wytschaete in the same way and to the same degree. In a brilliant manner, he was able to make the fullest and most conservative use of the combined forces – in accordance with the instructions of the *Gruppe* and corresponding to the tactical situation – where the decisive battle took place on the ground, always with the goal in mind of carrying out the destruction of the enemy. The downing of 84 aircraft by the *Jagdgruppe* bears witness to this.

'To all of the units he was a fair commander who placed the greatest demands on his own person. Utterly modest and militarily correct with respect to his superiors, popular with and admired by all his comrades.'

Staffelführer **Oblt Berthold displays the 'charming' side of his personality (as recalled by Walther Kleffel) in this pleasing study. On 10 October Berthold was grievously wounded yet again and just managed to land his riddled aircraft back at Harlebeke. He would be out of action for six months** (*Rahn collection, NMUSAF*)

On 14 October 1917 Strähle wrote that 'Klein flew his Pfalz D III for the last time'. It may have been replaced by this Albatros D V. Klein's personal marking of a white panel was capped with a segment of a darker, unknown colour around the cockpit. The future ace flew aggressively in October but did not achieve any victories. On the 20th Strähle wrote that the *Jasta* attacked five DH 4s and 'One, hit by Klein, started to smoke, spun down but recovered low down'. Klein would play a role in the eventful duel with No 28 Sqn on 26 October (*J Rief*)

Lt Theodore Vernon-Lord of No 84 Sqn is seen in his flight gear as fascinated pilots of *Jastas* 24 and 18 study his SE 5a B574. Vernon-Lord landed his machine on the airfield at Harlebeke on 15 October 1917. According to the *Jasta* 24 war diary, Lord was forced to land due to a broken pushrod that had damaged the crankcase (*Rahn collection, NMUSAF*)

As evidenced in this official evaluation, Berthold's impact on the performance of *Jasta* 18 cannot be overestimated. In his absence, acting command of the *Staffel* was given to Oblt Ernst Wilhelm Turck, the most senior regular army officer in the unit. As Berthold noted in his letter, 'Father' Turck was no high-scoring ace, but he had been a positive influence within the *Jasta*. It must be stated, though, that once Berthold was gone much of the unit's momentum left with him. The *Jasta* failed to chalk up a single confirmed victory during the rest of October and only one in November.

There was, nonetheless, still no shortage of aerial combats and other noteworthy incidents. In early October Strähle reported that during an afternoon's flight in a blanket of fog and rain, he narrowly missed colliding with Schober's machine – by two metres! On the 14th he recorded that 'Oblt Turck gets command of *Jasta* 18 and also becomes *Jagdgruppenführer* of *Jagdstaffeln* 18, 24, 33 and 36 replacing Oblt Berthold.'

On 15 October DH 4's of No 25 Sqn bombed the ammunition dump at Harlebeke, escorted by SE 5as from No 84 Sqn on that unit's very first combat mission. During their return flight the No 84 Sqn machines were strongly attacked by German fighters and SE 5a B574 was 'neatly landed' by 2Lt T Vernon-Lord on the Harlebeke airfield that *Jasta* 24 shared with Berthold's pilots. Once again the *Staffel* 18 pilots could examine this type in detail.

A patrol by nine *Jasta* 18 pilots at midday on 20 October resulted in a great deal of action with no tangible results. Near Ypres they encountered, 'An enemy formation of five DH 4s and several SPADs', according to Strähle's diary. 'Klein left the *Kette* and boldly attacked a SPAD without result (near Deulemont), and a Triplane patrol tried to engage us but did not press the attack'. These British aircraft may actually have been Nieuport 27s of B Flight, No 1 Sqn, along with a Sopwith Triplane from 1 Naval Squadron. They engaged nine enemy scouts over Linselles, and Capt Rogers of No 1 Sqn fired 60 rounds at a 'red nosed enemy aircraft' from a range of 20 yards and claimed it as out of control as his fifth of nine victories. Be that as it may, neither side suffered any fatal losses.

On 26 October, promising newcomer Ltn Hans Viebig was transferred in to *Jasta* 18 from *Jasta* 20. He had only flown with his previous *Staffel* since the beginning of the month but had already downed a Bristol Fighter on the 11th for his first *Luftsieg*. Viebig would not score again in *Jasta* 18, but was a steadfast flying comrade and valued member of the *Staffel*. He would later follow Paul Strähle to *Jasta* 57 and attain four more victories with that unit prior to being wounded on 30 June 1918.

AN EPIC COMBAT

26 October 1917 was a day on which nobody – German or British – should have been flying in Flanders. Heavy rains that started the previous night lasted throughout the day, but failed to prevent the British high command from launching yet another push into the sodden quagmire around Poelcapelle.

On the soggy RFC field at Droglandt, the Sopwith Camels of C Flight of the new No 28 Sqn were rolled out of their hangars into the light rain. The recently-appointed C Flight commander was Canadian Capt William George Barker, who was destined to survive the war as one of the most celebrated of all British aces with 50 victories. He would earn the Victoria Cross exactly one year and a day later in a legendary one-sided combat.

However, on this rainy Friday Barker had just one victory to his name, achieved six days earlier. He was nonetheless an extremely experienced flier, and eager to prove his appointment as a flight commander was merited. Barker had heard that the Richthofen Circus was across the lines at Marckebeeke. He went over his squadron commander's head and obtained permission to lead a group of volunteers on an aerodrome raid. Barker was not one to let bad weather cancel his plans, and reasoned it would increase the chances of surprising the enemy.

His volunteers included Lts N C Jones, J B Fenton and, most noteworthy, H S Malik. Hardit Singh Malik was the only Sikh pilot in the RFC. An honours graduate of Oxford, he wore a specially tailored outsize flying helmet that fitted over his turban. Having struggled against prejudice to get his commission, he was a dedicated and courageous pilot whom Barker called the 'Indian Prince'. Malik later recalled of the mission, 'It was a most foolhardy

In the postwar years, Capt William George Barker recalled his 26 October clash with *Jasta* 18 as 'my most thrilling sky fight', choosing it over his legendary VC combat against superior numbers. He is seen here in Italy as CO of No 139 Sqn with his equally famous Camel, B6313. He had earlier flown this machine in No 28 Sqn during the contest with *Jasta* 18

2Lt Hardit Singh Malik, the 'Flying Sikh', is seen with a Sopwith Camel at Yatesbury, in England. While serving with No 28 Sqn he flew with Barker against *Jasta* 18 and was wounded by Paul Strähle (*J Guttman*)

operation, and was planned over the CO's head. He actually forbade it, but Barker got the okay from Wing HQ'. Malik was game for whatever Barker offered.

At 1045 hrs the four Camels struggled to lift off from the mud at Droglandt and headed into the soft drizzle. At the same time four Albatros scouts took off from Harlebeke and headed into the 'showery strong southwest wind'. The German fighters were handled by four of the most seasoned *Jasta* 18 veterans, Paul Strähle (flying D V 4594/17), Otto Schober, Arthur Rahn and Johannes Klein. Rahn had arrived at the *Staffel* a mere six days before, but he was a veteran of ten months in *Jasta* 19 and had three confirmed claims to his name.

Soon after the RFC pilots started out, Jones became separated from his flight commander and then Fenton did as well – but Malik in Camel B5406 stayed glued to Barker's B6313 despite the terrible visibility. West of Roulers, the Albatros *Kette* blundered into the Camels of Barker and Malik. 'At about 1200 metres we fired at two enemy single-seaters', wrote Strähle. 'One [Malik] dived to fire at targets on the ground and I went after him. The other [Barker] was engaged by Klein and Schober. Rahn stayed with me'.

Strähle hung on to Malik's Camel like a terrier, as the Indian tried every trick he knew. Strähle wrote;

'In a tough dogfight lasting more than a quarter-of-an-hour, sometimes only a few feet off the ground, I fought the enemy scout as far as Ichteghem, where unfortunately I had to break off because my guns had jammed. For me this fight was the hottest and most exciting that I had in my whole fighting career. Apart from the good pilot, his machine was faster and more manoeuvrable than mine, to which must be added the low altitude, showers and rain. But for this I might have got him. Once I thought he would have to land, as he had a long trail of smoke, but it was not to be. I landed on the aerodrome at Ichteghem, where it was raining heavily.

'For the whole of the fight I had used full throttle (airspeed 200 km per hour), 1600 rpm. Three times we were down to ground level! His machine had a "5" next to the cockade on the left upper wing.'

Strähle failed to receive confirmation for a victory in this contest, but in actuality he had wounded his opponent. Running short of fuel and weak from blood loss, Malik lapsed into unconsciousness and crashed his riddled Camel in Allied territory. He later recovered and lived to the age of 90, frequently recounting the tale of how he was shot down by 'the famous Richthofen squadron' (sic).

Barker, meanwhile, fought a fierce duel with Otto Schober. His combat report stated;

'I sighted 15 enemy aircraft west of Roulers. I attacked one with a red nose, fought for 15 minutes and at 1000 ft got a burst of 30 rounds at 20 yards range, and the enemy aircraft went down in flames and crashed.'

'A second enemy aircraft [apparently Klein] attacked me. We fought for about ten minutes at heights varying between 50 ft and 500 ft over the wood midway between Roulers and Thielt. While fighting and turning to the right, I got a burst of 40 rounds into the enemy aircraft, which sideslipped, crashed and burst into flames on the ground.'

Despite Barker's graphic description, Klein escaped unscathed. Barker also wrote a more colourful account in a letter to his mother;

'I was patrolling with two of my flight about seven miles over when we ran into 15 of Germany's best scouts. I knew the wind was against us, and I also knew that unless I did awfully well I would never get back, so I turned and attacked a Hun painted red – their leader. We fought for 15 minutes and he flew very well. We tried every stunt and at last by doing a roll I got both guns on him at 20 yards and shot him down in flames. I was attacked by another, and after ten minutes – fighting almost on the ground – I got my two guns on him and down he went.'

Strähle's report offers a different perspective on Schober's demise at the hands of the Canadian ace;

'Ltn Schober was attacked almost vertically from below and shot down by the other Englishman who had spun away before. Schober himself was hit by several bullets and dived straight into the ground. I had again lost a good friend and comrade, who was generally liked by the whole *Staffel*.'

Barker's companion, Lt Fenton, attacked a column of lorries. He was wounded by AA fire but returned safely, as did Jones. Several years after the war, Barker recounted the tale of this combat to a 'pulp' magazine journalist, choosing it (like Strähle) as 'my most thrilling air fight'. The red noses of his opponents' aircraft left no doubt in Barker's mind

One participant in the 26 October scrap was Arthur Rahn, who at that time had achieved half of his eventual six victories. He is pictured in the cockpit of his *Jasta* 18 D V, marked with a personal emblem of a white-bordered band of white diamonds (*Rahn collection, NMUSAF*)

Johannes Klein fought it out with Barker in the dogfight of 26 October, and was apparently claimed for the Canadian's third victory. However, Klein escaped and would go on to achieve at least 14 more of his own victories for a total of 16. His *Staffel* comrade Ltn von Ziegesar described Klein's later marking as a 'white belly band'. The white panel seen on his D V here was topped with a panel of another colour that enclosed the cockpit (*J Rief*)

that he had experienced a run-in with 'Richthofen's Circus' and vanquished two of them.

Schober's body was recovered, and Richard Runge and Paul Strähle attended the ceremony when it was entrained for burial in his hometown of Gotha. A priest delivered a eulogy. With the cynical fatalism typical of many *Jagdflieger*, Runge muttered to Strähle, 'What a load of rubbish! Schober will turn in his coffin'. Then Runge expressed his hope that he himself would be shot down in flames so that such a farcical 'show' could not be arranged. 'But what of your family?' asked Strähle. Runge responded that his parents were separated, so 'Who cares?' It would not be long before Runge would get his fatal wish.

For the remainder of October, *Jasta* 18 seemed unable to come to grips with the enemy. Oblt Auffarth, after racking up his first five aerial triumphs, left the *Staffel* on the 20th to take command of *Jasta* 29, where he would bring his record to 26 victories by war's end. On 30 October the British offensive resumed, directed toward capturing Passchendaele village. Terrible weather conditions severely limited flying for the first week of November, but did not prevent Canadian troops from capturing Passchendaele on the 6th.

Although Oblt Turck commanded the *Jasta,* the more experienced Strähle had been leading his seven-aeroplane *Kette* in the air. This changed on 8 November, as Strähle dubiously recorded. 'From now on Oblt Turck, our *Staffelführer,* will lead our *Kette* in my place. He still has a lot to learn, but it will come'. On the next day, 'The *Kette* flew much too far southwards. Turck did not allow for the strong northwest wind

Otto Schober had been born in Johannesburg, South Africa, on 12 March 1890. A veteran and valued member of *Jasta* 18 with one confirmed claim, he met his end as the second victory of William George Barker (*P Grosz*)

Apparently having just returned from a thrilling dogfight, a *Jasta* 18 pilot stands in the cockpit of his Albatros D V to recreate his manoeuvres for an amused audience. The goggled pilot is not identified, but he just may have been Paul Strähle. The third onlooker from the right, in the colourful stocking cap, is probably Kleffel. Strähle relinquished leadership of his *Kette* to *Staffelführer* Turck in early November, with mixed results (*Rahn collection, NMUSAF*)

and then had to go looking for the lines'. On-the-job training was a luxury denied to *Jasta* commanders, and Turck was not living up to the standard set by Berthold.

The only victory recorded by *Jasta* 18 in November came on the 15th when Veltjens achieved his 9th by claiming an 'SE 5' over the Staden-Langemarck Road at 0950 hrs. However, there was no elation in the *Staffel* mess that evening. 'On 15 November on a front flight in which I could take part due to illness, we lost one of our best pilots, Ltn Runge', wrote Strähle. 'He was shot down in flames at Langemarck by an SE 5 (sic)'. While other accounts state that Runge's D Va 5253/17 was brought down by flak, it is almost certain that he fell to the guns of No 45 Sqn's Capt K B Montgomery, flying Camel B3929. Montgomery was credited with destroying an Albatros that broke apart in flames over Langemarck at 1035 hrs for his tenth claim. In later years, Strähle recalled that the eight-victory ace Runge had 'died as he wanted, in flames. A beautiful comrade'.

Meanwhile, in a hospital in far-off Berlin, Rudolf Berthold impatiently suffered through endless surgeries and painful therapy, eager to return to

Veltjens' mechanic Johann Rief mailed a postcard of this photograph to his parents, dated 8 October 1917, and identified everyone in the groundcrew in this view taken at Harlebeke. From left to right are Rief, Werkmeister Kleber, Ltn d R Veltjens, Domschke and Kurjan. Veltjens scored the *Jasta's* sole November victory on the 15th (*J Rief*)

the Front. On 4 November he received a welcome and surprising telegram from *Kogenluft* von Hoeppner;

'His Majesty *der Kaiser und König* has recognised your outstanding services as a fighter pilot and leader of your *Staffel*, and is pleased to promote you to hauptmann. With heartfelt congratulations on this evidence of the recognition from your highest commanders, I also wish that upon your full recovery you may once again participate in the battle for German aerial supremacy.'

Three days later another cable arrived from Berthold's closest ranking superior in the field, the *Kommandeur der Flieger* (*Kofl*) of the 4. *Armee*, Hptm Helmuth Wilberg. As a close associate and personal friend, Wilberg wrote in a comradely manner. His cable read in part;

'Dear Berthold,

'Above all I would like to give you my warmest congratulations on your promotion. I am pleased to hear that you are doing well and that you are being carefully attended to and, above all, are being cared for by your younger sister. In this way, your recovery will certainly progress splendidly.

'With all my heart, I beg that you do not think of coming out here again too soon! You would not be giving yourself or the Fatherland the best service in this way. We need you in the Spring, not the Winter! Instead, you would do better to toughen your surely weakened body for the difficult tasks of next year. We are doing well. Wytschaete is becoming a slow, but quiet, front for sure! Your good men are valiantly at work, just like before. On the ground everything is good and secure – swamp, rain and cloud are fine allies. The *Armee* hopes that you will return!'

CAMBRAI

The famous tank assault of the Battle of Cambrai erupted approximately 50 miles south of Ypres on 20 November, initiating a new chapter in the history of *Jasta* 18. As part of the response to the new offensive, the *Staffel* received orders to transfer from the 4. *Armee* to the 6. *Armee*. On the 24th the *Jasta* flew from Harlebeke to Houplin, south of Lille, alternately going

On 11 November, as *Jasta* 18 flew to the Cambrai front, Paul Strähle lost his bearings in D V 4594/17 and landed at Avesnes-le-Sec. He then flew to Gavoiseves and 'Landed at *Jasta* 5's aerodrome to the south of it, where the rest of my *Staffel* were waiting'. Strähle's Albatros and some other *Jasta* 18 D Vs are seen on the *Jasta* 5 airfield at Boistrancourt, with its famous hangars and the chimney from a sugar factory in the background

According to a caption in the von Buttlar album, these relaxed pilots were photographed at Avelin on what must have been a warm day in late December 1917. From left are Hermann Margot, Rahn, Veltjens and von Beaulieu-Marconnay *(Rahn collection, NMUSAF)*

above and below the strong storm clouds and showers. Their stay at Houplin was only temporary, for on the 28th they relocated to Avelin. This nomadic life resumed in a few days when they packed their bags and headed south to the Cambrai front. On 30 November, as the pilots struggled to get their bearings through the 'complete stratus cover', they eventually landed at *Jasta* 5's airfield complex at Boistrancourt/Carniéres.

Oblt Turck led his seven-man *Kette* on a front flight from Carniéres that same day. They encountered some SE 5as harrying a German bomber, but Strähle commented, 'Our *Kette* did not do very well, partly because of the leadership and partly owing to the cloud'. On a second flight on the 30th, they again engaged a flight of SE 5as, most likely from No 41 Sqn. Schäfer's Albatros was shot up and Hans Viebig got a bullet through his glove.

On 1 December two neophyte fighter pilots were posted to *Jasta* 18. One was NCO pilot Max Hitschler, who would not achieve greatness but who did survive the war. The other raw beginner was Ltn Oliver

Max Hitschler was posted to *Jasta* 18 on 1 December and is pictured here with his Pfalz D IIIa, which sported five vertical white rings as a personal emblem. This aircraft may in fact be something of a hybrid, as it is a D IIIa but retains the pointed lower wingtips generally seen on the D III *(P M Grosz)*

Albatros D V 2171/17 was the mount of Ltn Oliver *Freiherr* von Beaulieu-Marconnay in the winter of 1917-18. As a member of the Prussian 4th Dragoons, he marked his fighters with the unit's '4D' branding iron emblem. The uppersurfaces of both wings were painted in the blue *Staffel* colour (*J Rief*)

Freiherr von Beaulieu-Marconnay, who had been born into a Prussian military family in Berlin-Charlottenburg on 14 September 1898. He joined the *Dragoner-Regiment* Nr 4 *'von Bredow'* as a fahnenjunker in the summer of 1915 and fought on the Eastern Front. Whilst still only 17 he was promoted to leutnant in July 1916 and had won the Iron Cross 1st Class by year-end.

Von Beaulieu transferred to aviation in the summer of 1917, and had done the usual service in two-seaters prior to his posting to *Jasta* 18. The talkative and mischievous 'Beauli' immediately became a popular member of the *Staffel*, demonstrating his promise on his first patrol. The '4D' branding iron emblem of his cavalry unit, the Prussian 4th Dragoons, would identify all of his fighter aircraft. Although von Beaulieu would not score his first victory until May 1918 (after he had

Ltn von Beaulieu-Marconnay makes friends with a *Jasta* 18 mascot some time in the winter of 1917-18. 'Beauli' would score 25 victories, but his career ended on 18 October 1918 during his command of *Jasta* 19 in JG II. His Fokker D VII was mistakenly attacked by a *Jasta* 74 pilot and he was mortally wounded. On 26 October the Kaiser signed the document awarding the 'Blue Max' to the 20-year-old ace, who died two days later (*Rahn collection, NMUSAF*)

transferred to *Jasta* 15), he was destined to earn a fierce reputation as a proficient air fighter in *Jastas* 15 and 19 of *Jagdgeschwader* II. He would receive the *Pour le Mérite* with a total of 25 opponents downed just before his death on 26 October 1918.

At 1115 hrs on 15 December, von Beaulieu joined a *Kette* led by Turck and including Kleffel and Strähle. Over Gavrelle, the group dived out of the sun onto three Camels from No 43 Sqn. 'We kept together well as I throttled back', Strähle commented. 'One of us fired too soon. Kleffel almost ran into me, a wild dogfight developed – unfortunately without success. Over Willeval, Vimy, four SEs or Sopwiths started another dogfight. The Tommies could not do a thing and eventually had to retreat. Our *Kette* flew very well, especially von Beaulieu, who was on his first flight over the Front'. The second scrap was likely against an SE 5a formation from No 40 Sqn, with Capt J H Tudhope claiming an Albatros out of control over Douai for his fourth of ten victories.

At some point in mid-December the travels of the *Jasta* finally ceased as the unit settled in at Avelin, east of Seclin, for the next three months. Although aerial action was somewhat lessened, the skies over the 6. *Armee* were still dangerous. By 22 December, rookie pilot Ltn d R Hans Villinger had been with *Jasta* 18 exactly one day short of a month, but his time was up. He was part of a *Staffel* patrol that was jumped by five SPAD VIIs from No 19 Sqn south of Quesnoy. The RFC pilots submitted a group report;

'At 1420 hrs the SPAD formation engaged eight Albatros Scouts and a general "dogfight" ensued. During this fight Lt Fairclough fired at one machine which dived steeply away, and he was unable to follow it

Ltn d R Hans Villinger was shot down and killed by pilots from No 19 Sqn on 22 December 1917 (*Rahn collection, NMUSAF*)

Life in a *Jagdstaffel* certainly was not all aerial combat, for youthful German airmen knew how to enjoy themselves. This *Jasta* 18 *Kostümfest* is dated sometime in late 1917. The party is obviously in full swing with drinks all around, and mascot 'Bella' joining in the fun. Seated in the centre in the top hat is Veltjens, and to the right of him is Arthur Rahn. Standing at extreme right is Walther Kleffel, then an unknown pilot (about to empty his drink on Rahn's head), then von Beaulieu-Marconnay in the white hat (*Rahn album, NMUSAF*)

down. Lt Olivier at the same time fired at one enemy aircraft as he was coming down towards the formation, and saw it go down in a spin. Capt Bryson fired at the lowest of the formation, and after getting two on his tail shook them off and, turning, attacked others. During this general fight one enemy aircraft was seen to go down with thick black smoke coming from it.'

Villinger fell at Le Mesnil at 1530 hrs German time. He was the last casualty of *Jasta* 18 in 1917.

In late December Paul Strähle received exciting news. His many months of staunch service and seven victories were being rewarded with a command of his own. The *Kogenluft* plan to expand the German air

Three costumed participants of yet another party pose while an unknown 'spy' peeks in the window. It hardly seems possible that these three exuberant young men accounted for a combined 71 enemy aircraft. From left are von Beaulieu-Marconnay, Veltjens (doing his best Charlie Chaplin impression) and Rahn (*Rahn Album, NMUSAF*)

Five officers of *Jasta* 18 strike a quick pose in December 1917. From left to right are Viebig, Schäfer, Veltjens, Strähle and Kleffel. At the end of that year Strähle was posted to lead the new *Jasta* 57, and he would take Hans Viebig with him (*Rahn collection, NMUSAF*)

service in response to the United States' participation in the war (known as the *Amerika-Programm*) called for the formation of 40 new *Jagdstaffeln* by the spring of 1918.

Such a massive expansion required a host of new *Jasta* commanders as well, and Strähle had been tipped to lead the brand new Prussian *Jasta* 57. Of course, this meant he would have to leave his cherished *Jasta* 18 for new challenges. In addition, with his transfer, the detailed account of *Jasta* 18's activities supplied by his war diary comes to an end, and the record becomes much more sparse. As was customary, Strähle was allowed to take two pilots from his old unit with him to provide an experienced cadre for his new *Jasta*, which was made up mostly of neophytes directly out of flying school. He chose to take Ltn Viebig and Gefr Hitschler to *Jasta* 57, and they left *Jasta* 18 in late January 1918.

As the war's third year drew to a close, the men of Royal Prussian *Jagdstaffel* 18 may have looked back on their unit's first 12 months with pride. The *Jasta* had recorded approximately 70 confirmed victories in exchange for nine pilots killed in action, five more wounded and one

Hans Burckhard von Buttlar arrived at the *Jasta* in mid-January 1918. He captioned this photo as 'My Pfalz D III' in his album. It was marked with an emblem of the 'man-in-the-moon' smoking a pipe (*P M Grosz*)

Another view of von Buttlar's Pfalz D III in the early winter of 1918 provides a glimpse of the light-coloured underside, most like factory finish silver-grey. The shadow of the top wing, as well as the mechanic on the right, falls across the rudder (*P M Grosz*)

One of the ways Berthold instilled an *esprit de corps* in his unit was with the adoption of a uniform and flamboyant *Staffel* colour scheme. This Pfalz D III was photographed some time in the winter of 1917-18, sporting the full unit livery of dark blue fuselage, tail and upper wing surfaces with a red nose. The airman's personal marking consisted of the three white intertwined rings, possibly based on the logo of the Krupp Works. Although headgear and scarf hinder positive identification, the pilot looks a bit like Walther Kleffel – but that is not confirmed (*J Rief*)

taken prisoner. As noted, however, the departure of Berthold seems to have left the *Staffel* pilots adrift, and very few successes had come their way since the end of September. The deaths of the veterans Runge and Schober, along with the transfer of Auffarth and Strähle, had a serious impact on the unit's offensive capability.

Fortunately, however, some promising new blood was also transferred into the *Jasta* to fill the gaps. We have seen that von Beaulieu-Marconnay arrived at the beginning of December 1917 and quickly proved his mettle. Ltn Hans Burckhard von Buttlar was posted in from AFP 8 on 15 January 1918.

This nobleman was born in Lübeck on 4 July 1893, and had served in *Königlich-Preussisches Kurhessiches Jäger-Bataillon* Nr 11. He was the son of Oberst Rudolf von Buttlar, who had died of heart failure as CO of *Reserve-Infanterie-Regiment* Nr 82 on 20 January 1915. Commissioned a leutnant on 11 September 1913, Hans Burckhard's career in the air service began on 12 August 1915 with his posting to the Rumpler School at Müncheberg. His frontline flying would be carried out in many different types, from handy single-seaters to the giant Staaken VGO II multi-engine bomber.

Of greater eventual significance to the pilots of *Jasta* 18 was the arrival of another young nobleman, Georg von Hantelmann, from *Jastaschule* I on 6 February 1918. Born in West Prussia on 9 October

1898, von Hantelmann enlisted in the *Braunschweigisches Husaren-Regiment* Nr 17 in 1916. The death's head emblem of this elite hussar regiment would later adorn at least one of his aeroplanes. Service on both the Eastern and Western Fronts was rewarded with the Iron Cross 2nd Class on 26 April 1917. He was commissioned in June 1917 when still only 18.

Ltn von Hantelmann soon transferred to the *Fliegertruppe* and initiated his pilot training at a school at Hagenau, in the Alsace, on 20 September 1917, making his first solo on 13 November. He then received further instruction at FEA 9 in Darmstadt. On 30 January 1918 he was sent to *Jastaschule* I at Valenciennes for his final polishing before joining *Staffel* 18. Although he would score no confirmed victories during his stay in *Jasta* 18, von Hantelmann would carve his name into the record books by downing 29 opponents as a *Jasta* 15 sharpshooter in 1918, and narrowly miss out on his own *Pour le Mérite*.

The first two months of 1918 were surprisingly inactive for *Jasta* 18 and hardly an auspicious start to the year. Of course, part of this can be blamed on the onset of winter weather conditions that led to a slackening of aerial action all along the British Front. Strong winds, low clouds, rain and snow were prevalent. Indeed, for ten days from 7 to 16 February there was almost no flying at all.

The Battle of Cambrai had officially ended on 7 December, signalling the end of the offensives until the spring of 1918. Throughout January and February, the airmen of *Jasta* 18 flew occasional sorties when weather permitted and tried to stay warm, dry and well fed. Frontline rumours were flying about plans and preparations for a massive German operation in the spring. Yet, even the most clairvoyant of fortune-tellers could not have predicted the startling events that would overtake the *Jasta* in March of 1918.

Winter temperatures in early 1918 necessitated the heavy overcoats worn by three of these Jasta *18 pilots, with a backdrop of two Pfalz D IIIa machines. They are, from left to right, von Beaulieu-Marconnay, Kleffel, Dingel and von Buttlar. Perhaps they were eagerly anticipating the coming of better weather and the great Spring Offensive (*Rahn collection, NMUSAF*)*

TRANSFORMATION

T he first months of 1918 were a time of immense preparation by the German Army for its massive offensive known as 'The Great Battle of France', which would be launched in March. The Bolshevik Revolution of 1917 and the consequential armistice of 3 March 1918 would ensure that thousands of veteran German troops could be released from the Eastern Front to reinforce the western armies. It was decided to launch an attack on an lengthy front from just south of Arras in the north to La Fère in the south in the direction of Amiens in the hope that a wedge could be driven between the French and British armies. Advance elements of the assaulting German armies would then attempt to seize the Channel ports. The ultimate goal was to force Britain and France into defeat before men and resources from the USA could be brought over in enough numbers to decide the war in favour of the Allies.

The 17., 2. and 18. *Armees* were destined to undertake the main roles in the upcoming offensive. The German High Command (*Oberste Heeresleitung*, or *OHL*) determined that, among other aviation formations, each of the attacking armies should have a *Jagdgeschwader* at its disposal. Such a unit was a permanent grouping of four *Jagdstaffeln* under a permanent commanding officer who was directly responsible to the Army Headquarters (*Armee-Ober-Kommando*, or *AOK*).

Von Richthofen's *Jagdgeschwader* I (composed of *Jasta* 4, 6, 10 and 11) had proven its worth since its creation in June 1917, and it would be assigned to 2. *Armee.* Two other *Jagdgeschwader* were brought into being on 2 February 1918, in anticipation of the offensive. JG II was comprised of *Jagdstaffeln* 12, 13, 15 and 19, and was created in the 7. *Armee* sector under the command of the accomplished Bavarian Hptm Adolf Ritter von Tutschek. At the same time, *Jasta* 2 'Boelcke', 26, 27 and 36 were united to form JG III in the 4. *Armee,* commanded by Hptm Bruno Loerzer. During the offensive JG II was destined to advance with the 18. *Armee* while JG III would be assigned to the 17. *Armee.* The first phase of the titanic offensive, code-named Operation *Michael,* would be launched on 21 March.

While all of these preparations were being made, the airmen of *Jasta* 18 continued to fly their missions from Avelin in the 6. *Armee,* with disappointing results. In fact, the available war records of the *Staffel* for the first seven weeks of 1918 are virtually blank. Veltjens finally chalked up the first victory of 1918 on 18 February, when he claimed a Sopwith Camel brought down near Violaines at about 1230 hrs. Oddly enough it had also been Veltjens who achieved the previous victory for *Jasta* 18 way back on 15 November 1917.

Two victories in jut over 13 weeks hardly made for a creditable record. It must be said that under Oblt Turck's leadership the *Jasta* performance had been sadly under par. Then, finally, in early March came the news that must have gladdened the hearts of the old hands – the indomitable Berthold, now a hauptmann, was returning to *Jasta* 18.

Josef Veltjens scored *Jasta* 18's first victory since 15 November 1917 when he was credited with a Sopwith on 18 February 1918. The jacket he wears here, lined with a tiger skin, was a prized possession. He was still wearing it when he joined the *Freikorps* armoured vehicle unit *Tank Division Lüttwitz* in December 1918 to help crush the 'Spartakus' Revolt in Berlin (*A E Ferko*)

As his old commander Hptm Wilberg had told Berthold back in November, 'We need you in the spring, not the winter!' and so he gamely returned to offer his services in the great offensive. Yet when the seemingly indestructible Franconian arrived at Avelin, his ravaged right arm was still in a sling and the wounds still festered. Furthermore, *Kogenluft* von Hoeppner himself had forbidden him to fly. Thus, Berthold summoned a dear comrade from his days at FFA 23 and *Jasta* 4, the celebrated Oblt Hans Joachim Buddecke, to join him at *Jasta* 18. Like his friend,

In the period from the end of October 1917 until the *Kaiserschlacht* on 21 March 1918, *Jasta* 18 recorded only two victories. Both went to 'Seppl' Veltjens, whose Albatros D V is seen on a snowy field in early 1918 (*J Rief*)

Hauptmann Buddecke

Hans-Joachim von Buddecke was one of Berthold's oldest and closest friends, and was brought in from *Jasta* 30 to lead *Jasta* 18 in the air. Buddecke had gained his fame in the Dardanelles campaign, and is seen here in the uniform of a Turkish hauptmann in this Sanke postcard

The reunion of Berthold with the pilots of *Jasta* 18 and his old comrade Buddecke formed the occasion for a series of group photohraphs, taken between 8 and 10 March. These men are, from left to right, Turck, Dingel, Schäfer, von Beaulieu-Marconnay (facing left), Kleffel, von Hantelmann (note the death's head on his cap), Margot, Veltjens, Ltn d R Lohmann (*Jasta* OzbV), Rahn, Berthold (with right arm in a sling), von Buttlar, Buddecke, Theodor Weischer and Klein (*Rahn collection, USAFM*)

Buddecke wore the blue enameled *Pour le Mérite* at his throat. It was intended that he would lead the *Jasta* in the air until the *Staffelführer* was fit to fly.

Born into a military family in Berlin on 22 August 1890, Hans-Joachim Buddecke was commissioned in the *Leibgarde-Infanterie-Regiment* (1. *Grossherzoglich Hessisches*) Nr 115 in 1910. After leaving the army in 1913, he travelled to the USA and worked for his uncle's automobile firm in Indianapolis. His interest in aviation led him to purchase a Nieuport monoplane and teach himself to fly.

Upon the outbreak of war he managed to return home to join the *Fliegertruppe*, and was flying with his close friend Berthold in FFA 23 by September 1915. Flying a Fokker Eindecker, Buddecke scored his first victory on 19 September 1915, then two more in the next two months. Near the end of 1915 Buddecke was transferred to the Dardanelles, where he continued to fly Fokkers as part of the German Military Mission to aid the Turks. Despite the scaled-down scope of air activity in that distant theater, Buddecke attained at least four more victories in January 1916, along with several unconfirmed claims. On 14 April he became the third airman to receive the 'Blue Max' (after Immelmann and Boelcke). Then he returned to the Western Front and became the first commander of *Jasta* 4, where his path crossed with that of Berthold once again. He added three more victories in September to bring his total to ten, then returned to the Turkish theatre.

Buddecke remained in the East throughout most of 1917, scoring only two more times there before returning to France for the final great German offensive. However, his service in Turkey had not prepared him for the drastically altered, and advanced, state of aerial warfare on the Western Front. In order to acclimate himself to the new conditions he was posted to *Jasta* 30, not as the leader but as a regular pilot. It was with that unit that he was accorded his 13th, and last victory, a Sopwith Camel on 19 February. Then he got the call to come to *Jasta* 18 to assist his old flying mate Berthold.

Buddecke arrived at Avelin on 8 March 1918, and this event was commemorated with a series of photographs taken of the entire *Staffel*. Yet Berthold soon had cause to regret his request to his old friend. On 10 March Buddecke led a flight of *Jasta* 18 fighters out on a frontline

patrol, but he would never return. He was probably the victim of Canadian ace Flt Lt Arthur T Whealy of 3 Naval Squadron. The RNAS pilot was flying Camel B7220 at the head of his flight east of Lens at 10,000 ft. His combat report states that he spotted a group of Albatros fighters;

'I dived down with my flight on about seven or eight enemy aircraft. After pulling out of a dive on one enemy aircraft I saw another to my left about 500 ft below, heading away from me. I immediately dived on his tail and opened fire at about 100 yards, firing a burst of about 40 rounds from each gun. The enemy aircraft turned half over onto its back and went down in a series of stalls and spins. I watched it till it was about 3000-4000 ft above the ground and then lost sight of it on account of the haze, but I feel fairly certain that I hit the pilot. Other pilots of the patrol observed the enemy aircraft crash.'

A good shot bears repeating, so this excellent (and previously published) view from the *Jasta* 18 photo session is presented without apology. In the front row, left to right, are Margot, Schäfer, von Buttlar, Veltjens (with his arm on Buttlar's shoulder), Berthold (seated), Buddecke, Klein and Rahn. From left to right in the back row are an almost-hidden von Hantelmann, Lohmann, Turck, Dingel (arm in arm with Turck), Kleffel (behind Buddecke), Weischer and von Beaulieu-Marconnay shading his eyes (*Rahn collection, NMUSAF*)

On 10 March Hans-Joachim Buddecke was shot down and killed, most probably by Flt Lt Arthur T Whealy of 3 Naval Squadron. Whealy is seen here seated in a Camel and chatting with his fellow Canadian ace, and No 203 Sqn CO, Raymond Collishaw during later service

Although two other Camel pilots in this fight also claimed 'out of control' victims, it seems most likely that Whealy shot down Buddecke as the tenth of his 27 eventual victories. Buddecke fell at Harnes, east of Lens. His body was quickly recovered and he was buried in Berlin on 22 March.

On 15 March another redoubtable fighter ace of the *Luftstreitkräfte* met his end. About 100 kilometres south of *Jasta* 18's base at Avelin, the accomplished Bavarian Hptm Adolf Ritter von Tutschek was killed in his Fokker Dr I 404/17 at Brancourt. With his demise the German Air Service lost not only a respected and highly decorated pilot, but also a *Jagdgeschwader Kommandeur*. JG II was suddenly leaderless, less than a week before Germany's greatest offensive was scheduled to begin.

It had never been easy to find an officer qualified to lead a *Jagdgeschwader*, and the vacancy left by von Tutschek's death was a problematic one. The specifications for such a *Kommandeur* required that he be an active (regular) army officer – not an officer of the reserves – and preferably of hauptmann rank or higher. Certainly it was also desirable that the commander be a veteran and highly successful *Jagdflieger*. Such officers were few indeed, and it was inevitable that the eyes of *Kogenluft* should now turn to Hptm Berthold for leadership of JG II. Berthold had advocated the formation of such a permanent grouping of *Jagdstaffeln* in the manner of the earlier *Kampfgeschwader* formations as early as February 1917. He had already asked *Kogenluft* for the command of a *Jagdgeschwader* for the coming offensive, but at the time his severely compromised physical state and health had prevented this.

Now, Berthold's ultimate goal was realised. He would command a prestigious fighter wing in Germany's greatest single assault of the war. He duly took part in the funeral ceremonies for von Tutschek in Laon on 17 March 1918, solemnly marching with other notables behind the gun carriage that bore the ace's coffin to the train station for shipment to the *Waldfriedhof* in Munich.

There was one stumbling block to be dealt with before Berthold officially took command of *Jagdgeschwader* II, however. He had just returned to the men of his cherished *Jasta* 18, a close-knit group that he believed he had trained and led to a high level of performance. He did not want to leave them behind as he moved on to this new command. When he had been ordered to leave *Jasta* 14 to take over *Jasta* 18 some seven months before, Berthold had managed to bring four of his most

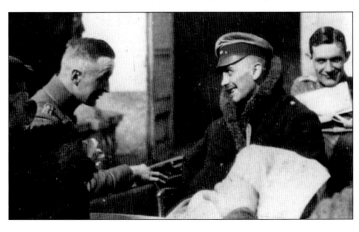

Hauptmann Berthold returned to his cherished *Jasta* 18 in the first week of March 1918, although he was still far from healthy. Here, Berthold smiles gamely from the back seat of his car, in spite of festering wounds in his right arm. A happy Josef Veltjens is seen just behind Berthold (*Rahn Collection, NMUSAF*)

trusted pilots and a few mechanics with him. Now, he would do this again but on a much larger scale.

Berthold reportedly made it a condition of his appointment as *Kommandeur* of JG II that he be allowed to transfer all the pilots and ground personnel from his old *Jasta* 18 to one of the component *Staffeln* of the *Geschwader*. The timing could hardly have been worse, for his request for this full-scale shift of personnel came on the eve of the great offensive. Such was the authority, and respect, granted to Berthold within the high command that on 20 March wholesale transfers of personnel took place between

Jasta 18 and *Jasta* 15 – the component *Staffel* of JG II that had been selected for the swap. Basically, what this amounted to was an exchange of numbers between the two units. To quote historian Alex Imrie;

'Despite the manner of its execution, as outlined in the War Diaries of both *Jasta* 18 and *Jasta* 15, whereby listed personnel are shown to be transferred from one unit to another, it was in fact a paper exercise that could best be described as "for *Jasta* 18 read *Jasta* 15". Thus it was merely a renumbering process and a complete interchange between these units took place.'

Apparently, the sole exception was Ltn Monnington, the *Jasta* 15 *Offizier zur besonderen Verwendung* (Ozbv) or adjutant, who was retained in *Jasta* 15 for a time in order to facilitate the transition. Not only personnel but also aircraft were exchanged. This astonishing swap of two entire *Staffeln* was even more remarkable as it came on the very eve of Operation *Michael*, as the first phase of the Spring Offensive had been code-named, and extensive timetables and plans were already in place for both units.

Most likely there was some resistance to this swap, and no little confusion, amongst Berthold's superiors. Some 56 years later one of the participants, Walther Kleffel, remembered it in his own way;

'With 18 and 15 it's like this. Shortly before the March 1918 offensive Berthold, who came back to us from a hospital back home, became commander of *Jagdgeschwader* II, to which *Jasta* 15 belonged. Because Berthold didn't want to do without his old comrades, he simply switched the flying personnel – without permission to do so – for his men in *Jasta* 18 without a moment's hesitation, which led to a lot of confusion and of course great annoyance on the part of the *Kogenluft,* whose lists got all mixed up. In the end one just let the matter go through. So all the fliers who came to *Jasta* 18 in March belonged to *Jasta* 15 and conversely those who had come to 15 belonged to 18.'

Jagdgeschwader II had relocated to Guise airfield in the 18. *Armee* sector on 19 March, and it was there that the 'swap' was effected the next day. The 'old' *Jasta* 15, commanded by Ltn d R August Raben, moved to the

Hans Burckhard von Buttlar was one of the *Jasta* 18 airmen who took part in the swap of personnel on 20 March. After Max Hitschler left *Jasta* 18 for *Jasta* 57 on 28 January, his striped Pfalz D IIIa was taken over by von Buttlar, who had the white stripes painted over with a new marking. The hunting horn emblem was based on the crest of the helm in the von Buttlar family coat-of-arms (*A E Ferko*)

The Pfalz D IIIa of von Buttlar displayed his hunting horn insignia against a dark band that obliterated the white stripes that had been applied by Hitschler. This dark band may have been red (or a very dark blue or black). This Pfalz was transferred to *Jasta* 15 along with its pilot, and shows up in later line-up photographs (*A E Ferko*)

aerodrome at Bruille, east of Douai in the 17. *Armee* sector and took up the *Jasta* 18 title. As part of JG II, this unit had begun re-equipping with a few Fokker Dr Is, but it seems likely that most of these were left behind at JG II and the *Staffel* remained equipped with Albatros and Pfalz machines. With Ltn d R Raben came Ltn Kurt Monnington, Karl Albert Mendel, Erich Spindler, Hans Müller, Hans Schultz, Kurt Baier, Claus von Waldow, Bergner and Hebler, as well as NCO pilots Wilhelm Kühne, Richard Schleichardt, Mäurer and Glatz.

Coming to the 'new' *Jasta* 15 in JG II with Berthold were Oblt Turck, Ltn Veltjens, von Hantelmann, von Buttlar, von Beaulieu-Marconnay, Schäfer, Rahn, Dingel, Joachim von Ziegesar (who had only arrived at *Jasta* 18 on 15 March), Kleffel, Lohmann and NCO pilots Margot, Klein and Weischer. Thus, at this point Berthold's band of hunters and their red-nosed bluebirds leave the topic of this book. They went on to further successes, and tragedies, with JG II (see *Osprey Aviation Elite Units 19 – Jagdgeschwader Nr II Geschwader 'Berthold'* for further details).

STAFFEL RABEN

As the men and aircraft under August Raben's command arrived at Bruille airfield, the ill luck that had plagued the 'old' *Jasta* 18 for three months seemed to now attach itself to the 'new' *Jasta* 18 with depressing punctuality. On the very day of the exchange, 20 March, *Staffelführer* Raben was taking off from Bruille when his aircraft overturned. He broke his arm in the crash and left for a hospital in Marle to have the bone set and to convalesce. During his absence the *Jasta* was apparently placed under the acting command of Ltn Rodde, the OzbV.

Although his first day as leader of his unit under its new title of *Jasta* 18 hardly proved auspicious, Ltn d R August Raben was an able and inspiring commander. A pilot and leader of wide-ranging experience, he would soon return to lead his *Staffel* to better days. Born on 2 December 1892, Raben had first served in the 2. *Thüringisches Feldartillerie-Regiment* Nr 55. His distinguished service in the field artillery earned him the prestigious Ducal Saxe-Ernestine House Order on 22 March 1916.

On 18 April he transferred to the air service. After pilot training his first aviation combat assignment was with *Kampfstaffel* 25 of *Kampfgeschwader* 5 in August 1916. On 1 January 1917, the *Kampfgeschwader* were dissolved and their *Staffeln* were redesignated as *Schutzstaffeln* (*Schusta*) or protection/escort squadrons. Raben's unit became *Schusta* 7, and he continued to fly with it until the end of January, when he converted to fighters. His first such assignment was to *Jasta* 36 on 17 February 1917.

After gaining valuable experience with that unit, he was transferred to the new *Jasta* 39 as *Staffelführer* on 2 August 1917. Soon after he formed this new unit it was selected as one of three *Jagdstaffeln* that were to be sent to the Isonzo Front in Italy to bolster the Austro-

Hugo Schäfer, seen here in his *Jasta* 18 Albatros D V emblazoned with his white snake emblem, was another of the airmen involved in the switch with *Jasta* 15 in JG II. Like von Beaulieu-Marconnay, von Hantelmann and Veltjens, Schäfer's success rate would quickly accelerate in the summer of 1918 once he began flying the D VII. He survived the war with 11 victories (*J Rief*)

Hungarian forces. It was there that Raben appropriately achieved the first successes of his squadron, when he shot down two Caproni bombers on 26 September. *Jasta* 39 performed admirably under Raben's leadership, notching up 25 victories in just six weeks. Then Raben was seriously wounded by anti-aircraft fire at Ste Dona de Piava on 17 November 1917, and left for the hospital. He returned to the Western Front in time for the great Spring Offensive, and was placed in command of *Jasta* 15 on 14 March 1918, just six days before the swap with Berthold's group.

With or without Raben in command, *Jasta* 18 played its part in the *Kaiserschlacht,* or imperial battle, as General der Infanterie Ludendorff termed the first phase of the Great Battle in France. The offensive erupted on 21 March, a day of poor weather and low clouds. Most aerial activity in the 17. *Armee* was restricted until nearly midday due to the foggy conditions. The next day *Jasta* 18 was airborne, but it lost Ltn d R Hans Schultz. Although he was listed as missing, Schultz had in fact been shot down into the shell-torn area in the zone of the advancing German troops and was unhurt. He managed to evade capture and found his way back to the *Staffel* two days later.

It is possible that the 'new' *Jasta* 18 had run afoul of 3 Naval Squadron once again. C Flight's Camel pilots, led by Flt Cdr F C Armstrong, claimed three Albatros scouts destroyed near Marquion on the 22nd. Besides Armstrong, both Flt Sub-Lts Whealy and Pierce also claimed scouts shot down over the frontlines of the battlefront.

By the fifth day of the offensive – 25 March – the German assault troops had made great advances and the situation for the defending British forces was desperate. The call went out for every available RFC squadron to fly at low heights and attack the enemy with bombs and machine guns. Maj-Gen Salmond made his famous order to the 9th Wing which read, in part 'squadrons will bomb and shoot up

Once the great swap of personnel and equipment was complete, Ltn d R August Raben would lead the 'new' *Jasta* 18. Raben is pictured with his Albatros D III during his earlier days in *Jasta* 36 at St Loup in the summer of 1917. His short, fur-trimmed leather coat would be worn throughout the war. Raben's start as leader of *Jasta* 18 was anything but auspicious, for he was injured in a crash on the same day he exchanged commands with Berthold (*A E Ferko*)

Vzfw Mäurer was one of Raben's pilots who made the switch from *Jasta* 15 to 18. On the fourth day of the Spring Offensive, 25 March, he participated in an attack on low-flying Camels of No 80 Sqn and made an unsuccessful claim for one of them. He is seen here in the summer of 1918 with D VII (OAW) 2144/18 (*A E Ferko*)

Vzfw Wilhelm Kühne notched up the first victory of the newly redesignated *Jasta* 18 by downing a Camel on 25 March. This NCO pilot would go on to become one of the stars of *Staffel* Raben. His arm patch was applied during his service in FFA 56 (*N Franks*)

everything they can see on the enemy side of this line. Very low flying is essential. All risks to be taken. Urgent'.

These low-level flights were hazardous in the extreme and the valiant British airmen suffered heavy casualties. The pilots of *Jasta* 18 took advantage of the situation and ended their unit's long drought. On the 25th, Vzfw Kühne and Mäurer participated in an attack on two low flying Camels of No 80 Sqn south of Bapaume. It seems Kühne accounted for Camel C6724, which was captured along with its wounded pilot 2Lt G Miller – he died in captivity six days later. Vzfw Mäurer also claimed a Camel (possibly No 80 Sqn's B9223, 2Lt Radcliff killed) but failed to receive confirmation. Nonetheless, *Staffel* Raben had its first accredited *Luftsieg* under its *Jasta* 18 designation, and Kühne had his all-important number one.

Wilhelm Kühne had been born on 11 December 1888, and thus was older than most of his fellow pilots. Following service in *Grenadier-Regiment* Nr 10, he transferred to the flying service in late 1913. After flying with FFA 14 and 56, he took fighter training at *Jastaschule* Warschau. He wound up in *Jasta* 29 on 15 February 1917, and made his first claim on 12 May, but it remained unconfirmed. He then flew in the home defence unit *Kest* 9. In January 1918 he

Ltn d R Hans Müller had already achieved two victories when he took part in the exchange of pilots between *Jagdstaffeln* 15 and 18. On 27 March he claimed an RE 8 for the third of his eventual total of 12 confirmed claims (*A E Ferko*)

came to *Jasta* 15, and was destined to become one of the leading lights of *Staffel* Raben.

The next day *Jasta* 18 was again active over the raging battle, but this time Ltn Claus von Waldow was struck by ground fire near the Bapaume-Cambrai road. Although he made it back to the German lines, his severe leg and jaw injuries signalled the end of his war. Both his feet were later amputated and he was discharged in September.

The hot fighting concordant with the ongoing offensive continued on 27 March. One of the leading veterans of *Staffel* Raben, Ltn d R Hans Müller, was credited with downing an RE 8 north of Bapaume, between the lines, for his third victory. However, Müller's own machine was badly damaged by the RFC observer's defensive fire, and he was forced down in no-man's land (near Miraumont) just as Schultz had been five days before. Like Schultz, Müller succeeded in making it back to friendly lines. It is likely that he had engaged a No 59 Sqn machine, RE 8 B7722, flown by 2Lt Christian and Lt Hanning. Their aircraft had its controls shot up by a single enemy scout, and they crash-landed safely at Marieux, but claimed that they had shot down their attacker who crashed at Grandecourt.

As the offensive continued *Jasta* 18 resumed its wandering. On 8 April the pilots and aeroplanes moved back to Avelin in the 6. *Armee*, where they were hosted by the personnel of *Jasta* 41. On the 12th the unit's ground and support personnel moved north to Faches, near Lille (also in the 6. *Armee*, only eight kilometres north of Avelin), where they established quarters and put up their tent hangars. Soon they were joined by the pilots and their machines, and *Jasta* 18 was settled in as a whole unit again. On 14 April the entire *Staffel* was pleased to welcome Ltn d R Raben back to the fold, and the *Jasta* was truly complete.

It had relocated to the 6. *Armee* sector in order to participate in Ludendorff's second Spring Offensive, code-named Operation *Georgette* by the Germans and known as the Battle of the Lys to the British. On the morning of 9 April the 6. *Armee* launched a massive attack between the La Bassée Canal and Armentières. The mist and rain which accompanied the assault made aerial cooperation hazardous, but the German storm troops swept through the Portuguese-held portion of the British line and advanced through the breach, crossing the River Lys at Bac St Maur. The next day, to the north, the 4. *Armee* launched its attack against the British Second Army near Messines Ridge. The offensive continued through the days that followed, with the most intense air fighting being centred around Estaires and Neuf Berquin on the 12th.

On 21 April the entire *Luftstreitkräfte* was stunned to hear that JG I commander Manfred von Richthofen was missing in action in the Somme Valley. That same day *Jasta* 18 suffered its own casualty when Vzfw Mäurer was sent to the hospital with severe wounds in the knee and upper leg – he would return to the *Jasta* several months later. The loss of Mäurer was balanced somewhat by the success of Vzfw Glatz, who successfully claimed a SPAD at 1530 hrs north of Froyelles for his first victory. On 29 April the offensive in Flanders culminated in a final push between Locre and Ypres, but the attack was a failure and the last Ludendorff offensive on the British front ended. The month of April

On 21 April 1918, Vzfw Glatz obtained his one and only confirmed victory when he brought down a SPAD at Froyelles. He is seen here later in the summer of 1918 in front of a D VII bearing the raven *Staffel* emblem and two vertical dark-coloured bands as personal insignia

concluded with yet another change of location for *Jasta* 18, this time the unit heading 12 kilometres northwest to Lomme airfield, west of Lille. It remained in the 6. *Armee*, however.

RAVENS TRIUMPHANT

Once *Staffel* Raben settled in for what would be a six-week stay at Lomme, the unit entered upon its most successful month since the glory days of the 'old' *Jasta* 18 back in September. Under Raben's capable leadership the squadron reached a cohesion and efficacy that it had not experienced for some time.

As part of his effort to facilitate an *esprit de corps,* Raben – like Berthold before him – instituted a flamboyant colour scheme for the unit's aeroplanes that would identify them to friend and foe alike. The Albatros

Unfortunately, neither the location nor the date of this rare photograph of three *Jasta* 18 fighters is recorded, but it is still worthy of study. At the right is a Pfalz D IIIa in full unit livery and, oddly, a man-in-the-moon motif similar to that seen on von Buttlar's Pfalz D III. However, it is not confirmed that this Pfalz was flown by von Buttlar, nor does it appear in his album. Next is an OAW-built Albatros D III that is believed to have been flown by Oblt Turck, bearing a narrow black band bordered by two broad white bands. Finally, another D III displays a chevron emblem (*R Kastner*)

This splendid Albatros D Va provides a good look at the famous black raven emblem inspired by the CO, August Raben. The nose and probably the uppersurface of the top wing were painted a bright vermilion, which was extended to border the cockpit rim. The lower wing was not painted red in this case, but remained in factory finish of printed five-colour 'lozenge' fabric. The unknown pilot's insignia consisted of the three-pointed 'Mercedes' star. Many will note that this was the same emblem later employed by Heinz Küstner on his D VII. However, Küstner only arrived at *Jasta* 18 on 7 July, well after the Albatros fighters were gone. The pictured airman does not especially resemble Küstner (*P M Grosz*)

D Va and Pfalz D IIIa aircraft were decorated with white tails and fuselages from the cockpit aft. The noses were painted a bright vermilion red, set off with a white propeller spinner. In many cases the upper surfaces of the top wings were painted red as well (later this would also apply to the lower wings), providing a vivid display. Even more distinctively, the aircraft were marked with a pictorial unit insignia in the manner more associated with French *escadrilles* or American squadrons, but rarely seen among the *Jagdstaffeln*.

Since the unit was informally known as '*Staffel* Raben', which translates as the ravens squadron, each aircraft was emblazoned with the black silhouette of a raven on the fuselage, just below and behind the cockpit. *Staffelführer* Raben had used a similar insignia as a personal marking on his aircraft in *Jasta* 39. In *Jasta* 18, each pilot also personally identified his aircraft with an individual emblem on the fuselage, sometimes supplemented by a pattern of coloured stripes on the horizontal stabiliser. Ltn Raben himself had managed to acquire a Fokker Dr I triplane for his personal use (possibly retained from *Jasta* 15 after the big personnel swap), and this machine also displayed the *Staffel* colours. The aircraft would eventually be marked with a white raven on the red portion of the fuselage as the commander's own distinctive badge.

Equipped with such resplendent fighters, the pilots of *Jasta* 18 set out to make their mark. May's impressive victory streak started on the 3rd, when Ltn der Landwehr Karl Albert Mendel was credited with downing a DH 4 northeast of Steenwerck at 1530 hrs for his third confirmed claim. Born on 4 October 1892 in Jerichow, Mendel had joined *Jasta* 15 in April 1917. There he had learned the trade of a

Jagdflieger from such worthy role models as Heinrich Gontermann and Ernst Udet. On 13 August 1917, Mendel flamed a French balloon for his first victory, which was followed by a French two-seater on 23 October. Five months later he was part of the mass transfer of pilots to *Jasta* 18.

4 May 1918 was a momentous day for the *Staffel*. At about 1850 hrs, five of the red and white fighters engaged a flight of Camels from No 4 Sqn of the Australian Flying Corps (AFC) above Vieux Berquin. Leading the *Jasta* 18 *Kette* was the redoubtable Hans Müller,

and fortunately his combat report from this fight survives. He was flying Albatros D Va 7387/17, which he described as having a 'red and white fuselage, black and white band, streamer on tail' (he had applied his usual personal marking of a fuselage band with diagonal black/white stripes). In requesting confirmation of his fourth victory from the *Kofl* of the 6. *Armee*, Müller wrote;

Karl Albert Mendel had two victories before the personnel swap of 20 March, and downed his third adversary on 3 May 1918. He is seen here during his previous service in *Jasta* 15. In common with contemporary Albatros fighters of the unit, his D V featured roughly applied two-tone camouflage on the fuselage. His personal embellishments included a large 'M' painted on the fuselage above a bird emblem, two vertical stripes and a '2' beneath each wing

Staffel Raben obtained a trio of confirmed claims on 4 May for its best day yet. One of the victors was Hans Müller, who was flying Albatros D Va 7387/17 when he destroyed a Camel. Müller earlier flew a Pfalz D IIIa from mid-April to May, and survived the harrowing incident documented by this photograph. The shattered propeller and damage around the engine may have resulted from a malfunction of the machine gun synchronisation system, or possibly from flak. Whatever the cause, Müller was lucky to land the crippled Pfalz safely

Lomme airfield, which was bombed by the RAF on 18 May, is probably the location featured in this photograph of ten fighters of *Staffel* Raben. At the head of the line is Raben's own Fokker Dr I in red and white, with the wing crosses on white fields – this triplane would later have a white raven emblem added to the red portion of the fuselage. The rest appear to consist of Albatros D Va machines, with the third aircraft from the left bearing the black skull and crossbones emblem favoured by Kurt Monnington. The fourth aircraft from the left was marked with black/white stripes and a bird emblem (slightly different from the unit marking) on the white fin. As Ltn d R Raben had earlier employed a similar version of a raven emblem on his *Jasta* 39 Albatros, this aeroplane might have belonged to the *Staffelführer* at some point. At the distant end, a Hannover CL type two-seater 'hack' machine is just visible, with its fuselage painted in the unit's red and white colours (*P M Grosz*)

'On 4 May at 1850 hrs, I with four machines attacked an equally strong flight of Sopwith Camels – one of which showed a large "B" on the upper right wing – northeast of Nieppe Wood at a height of 400 metres. After a short dogfight I shot the aircraft down in flames. It hit the ground on our side of the lines close to the northeast exit from the village of Vieux-Berquin and burned for about a quarter-of-an-hour.'

Müller's unfortunate opponent was Lt B W Wright, an Englishman attached to No 4 Sqn AFC, who died in Camel B5629.

In the same scrap Schultz also claimed a Camel for his first victory and Mendel added another to bring his score to four – although No 4 Sqn suffered no other losses. Not to be outdone, two of the Camel pilots also claimed to have downed Albatros scouts out of control, but *Jasta* 18 had no known casualties.

On 11 May *Jasta* 18 chalked up three more sucesses, this time over SE 5as. Richard Schleichardt downed a British fighter at Dranoutre at about 1820 hrs. Five minutes later Kurt Monnington brought down another SE 5a near Bailleul for his first victory, while Mendel did the same to 'make ace'. It would seem that the *Jasta* 18 pilots first encountered a patrol from No 1 Sqn, which was then joined by more aircraft from 41 Sqn. No 1 Sqn's Lt Pelletier was shot down in flames over Bailleul, and a few minutes later No 41 Sqn's Lt Stacey was wounded in the foot when his SE 5a was shot up.

The airmen that *Jasta* 18 had been fighting for the past several weeks were no longer part of the RFC – a fact that would have mattered little to the German pilots had they known it. On 1 April 1918, the RFC and RNAS had been combined into the new Royal Air Force (RAF), the world's first totally independent air arm. On Saturday, 18 May, the RAF demonstrated its increasing might in a bomb raid on the airfield at Lomme, home of both *Jastas* 18 and 47. At about 1430 hrs, DH 9 bombers of No 206 Sqn appeared over the aerodrome and began

This poor quality but rare photograph depicts the Albatros D Va pictured fourth from left in the preceding line-up shot, although at a somewhat later date. The unit's red and white colours were applied to fuselage and wing uppersurfaces. The bird emblem(?) that once appeared on the fin has curiously been removed or painted over in intense, opaque white. The five black/white stripes in the proportion of the Iron Cross ribbon composed the pilot's personal emblem. Note the early D VII in the background

dropping their ordnance. Ten aircraft of *Staffel* Raben were lightly damaged. *Jasta* 47 got the worst of it, losing three tents and a single Pfalz D IIIa to flames, with three other machines slightly damaged, and three mechanics wounded.

The raid hardly seems to have slowed *Jasta* 18 down, however, for on 22 May Müller downed a SPAD at Estaires at 1035 hrs and Gefr Deberitz recorded another at Fleurbaix 20 minutes later. This time the Albatros pilots were up against a new kind of foe, for they had tangled with the 103rd Aero Squadron of the nascent US Air Service (USAS). The 103rd was a unit originally formed from pilots of the famous SPA124 *Lafayette Escadrille*. The squadron, with its SPAD VIIs and XIIIs still identified by the famous Sioux Indian head emblem, had moved to Leffinckroucke on the Belgian coast on 5 May, bringing them within the area of *Jasta* 18's operations.

At about 1000 hrs on the 22nd, 1Lt Paul F Baer (in SPAD VII 3173) led four other pilots of the 103rd deep into German territory southwest of Armentières. A veteran of *escadrille* SPA80, Baer was one of the top

Americans of the 103rd Aero Squadron encountered *Jasta* 18 on 22 May and got the worst of it. Capt James Norman Hall poses with a Bleriot-built SPAD XIII of the 103rd, marked with the famous Sioux Indian head. This is thought to be SPAD No 2282, which Lt E A Giroux was flying when he was killed by Hans Müller on 22 May

aces of the USAS at the time with eight victories. At 5000 metres the Americans spotted six German single-seaters beneath them. Just as they dove on the scouts, they saw two or three other red-nosed fighters of *Jasta* 18 above them. Nonetheless, Baer – together with 1Lts E A Giroux and C H Wilcox – attacked the lower formation as the top cover from *Staffel* Raben sprung the trap and plunged into the fight.

Hans Müller fastened on to SPAD XIII 2282 and shot it down to a fiery crash, killing Giroux. Baer claimed to have shot down an Albatros in flames (although *Jasta* 18 lost no one) but had his controls severed by a burst from the fighter flown by Deberitz. Two of the *Jasta* 18 Albatros pilots pursued Baer all the way to the ground from 4000 metres. 1Lt George Turnure, one of the 103rd pilots, provided his own perspective on the fight in a letter;

'We flew quite far into the German lines. Lille was almost beneath us. Suddenly we encountered a patrol of six Boche *chasse* machines flying a few hundred metres below us and two of them above us. Our leader and two others attacked, diving down on the Boches below. I, being high man, stayed up as a guard and waited. Our men who attacked went down too far, and in turn were set upon by the Huns. So I from my advantageous position chose the highest of them and dove. In trying to escape me he went down like a crazy man and I had to dive almost vertically, full motor, in order to catch him.'

Turnure claimed to have shot down the German fighter but did not obtain confirmation.

Meanwhile, Paul Baer survived the devastating crash of his aircraft with a broken knee, and by his own account was taken prisoner and well treated at the airfield of *Jasta* 18 before he was taken off to a lengthy and difficult captivity. Later that same day, Wilhelm Kühne claimed a British fighter, but his claim was not upheld due to a lack of witnesses. The 'Yankee' airman that the pilots of *Staffel* Raben entertained that day must have been a source of great curiosity, for Baer was the first American they had encountered. He would not be the last.

For the remainder of the month, however, the hunters of *Jasta* 18 met only their traditional British opponents. At about 1245 hrs on 25 May they participated in a large dogfight west of Carvin, reportedly against 30 RAF aircraft. This was apparently a brawl with some seven Bristol Fighters of No 22 Sqn as well as a large formation of DH 4s from No 18 Sqn. *Jasta* 18's Richard Schleichardt forced what he described as an 'SE 5a' down behind Allied lines west of Lens but he was denied confirmation. His opponent may actually have been one of the DH 4s from No 18 Sqn, the crew of 2Lts Waugh and Walker having to force-land their badly riddled machine in a ploughed field near Houdain. In their turn, the No 22 Sqn crews put in claims for five enemy fighters shot down, while one of the No 18 Sqn crews was credited with an Albatros and Fokker Dr I out of control.

On 27 May the third Ludendorff offensive was opened on the French front on the Aisne, far to the south of *Jasta* 18's area – but *Staffel* Raben's operations against the RAF continued. On 28 May, Ltn Kurt Baier obtained his first and only confirmed victory when he shot down a 'DH 4' in flames near La Gorgue at 1120 hrs. This was, in reality, most likely Bristol F 2B C4763 from No 20 Sqn, flown by

The pilots under Raben's command made the most of their mediocre Albatros and Pfalz fighters in May 1918, obtaining successes against superior aircraft such as the SPAD XIII and Bristol F 2B. This rare view shows several Albatros D Va machines, including the one marked with a 'Mercedes' star seen in a prior photograph. Behind this machine a Pfalz D IIIa is visible, its white fuselage bearing only the *Staffel* raven emblem and no personal insignia (*E Lambrecht*)

Lts R G Bennett and G C Salter MC. The RAF airmen were both killed this day near Neuf Berquin. Bennett had been credited with nine victories prior to his demise.

29 May saw Wilhelm Kühne indulge in a bit of 'balloon fever' for what would be the first of four gasbags he would eventually destroy. He went after the British balloon of the 40th Section, 11th Company, 1st Balloon Wing near Thiennes and Nieppe Wood and succeeded in burning it. This was credited as his second victory in the *Nachrichtenblatt.*

As the month of May closed, the 'Ravens' of *Jasta* 18 could look back with satisfaction, for their exploits had clearly proved their mettle. They had claimed 11 aeroplanes and one balloon while sustaining no losses.

Even better, the *Staffel* was beginning to re-equip with a superior new aircraft – the superb Fokker D VII, which many historians consider to have been the best fighter of the Great War. When time permitted, the new Fokkers were suitably decorated in the dazzling red and white *Staffel* colours. The pilots of *Jasta* 18 looked ahead to the good flying days of summer 1918 with growing self-assurance.

June opened promisingly on the 1st when Ltn d L Mendel was credited with destroying a British aircraft near Laventie at about 1610 hrs, which brought his personal bag to six. The next day, the aggressive and persistent Wilhelm Kühne forced an enemy two-seater down near Nieppe Wood, but this was only credited as 'forced to land' and the unlucky NCO was again denied full credit for a claim. A similar *zur Landung gezwungen* record was achieved by Ltn d R Monnington on 3 June as he forced a DH 4 down at 0925 hrs near La Bassée, apparently within enemy lines.

Karl Albert Mendel had better luck on 4 June when an RE 8 went down in flames under his guns near Canveseure at 1520 hrs. This was probably E38 of No 4 Sqn, which was lost along with its crew of Lt Maltby and 2Lt Simms. This was Mendel's seventh victory, making him the most successful pilot in *Jasta* Raben. About two hours after Mendel got his RE 8, Kühne flamed another British balloon at Steenbecque for his third accredited claim – it was from the same unit as the one he had burned only six days previously. At about the same time Schleichardt claimed an Armstrong-Whitworth FK 8 two-seater but failed to obtain confirmation.

Three more claims on 5 June confirmed the increasing potency of *Staffel* Raben. At about 1205 hrs, Monnington was credited with a Bristol Fighter north of Violannes for his second victory. Just five minutes later Wilhelm Kühne brought down a British single-seater in Allied lines near La Bassée, which was confirmed as his fourth. That evening at about 2025 hrs, Ltn Hebler drove an RAF two-seater to the ground at Givenchy near La Bassée, but it was not confirmed and noted merely as another 'aircraft forced to land'.

BLACK THURSDAY

Jasta 18's uninterrupted string of successes came to an abrupt end during the evening of 6 June when nine of the unit's vermilion and white fighters were sent to patrol north of Hazebrouck at about 4000 metres. Most of them were probably the new Fokker D VIIs, which was a type still unfamiliar to the RAF. At about 1845 hrs they sighted a formation of SE 5as and dived to the attack. However, the experienced pilots from No 29 Sqn turned the tables on their opponents. Lts Rolfe, Reed and Ross filed this joint combat report;

'Five out of nine Pfalz (sic) Scouts dived on O P (offensive patrol) led by Capt R C L Holme MC at about 1745 hrs – height 13,000 ft. Lt Rolfe got on the tail of one and fired about 150 rounds at close range, following the enemy aircraft down to 9000 ft. Volumes of smoke started issuing from the enemy aircraft, which later caught fire and went down out of control, on fire. Lts A E Reed and C G Ross fought one enemy aircraft from 13,000 ft down to 1000 ft. The former fired 250 rounds and the latter 150 rounds from close range. The enemy aircraft went down out of control and was seen to crash by Lt T S Harrison northwest of Estaires at about 1800 hrs.'

In this combat *Jasta* 18 lost its most accomplished pilot, Karl Albert Mendel, who went down to a fiery end – probably under Rolfe's guns. In spite of the British pilots' identification, it is likely that Mendel was in a D VII. At the same time, No 29 Sqn's Lt Lagesse, in SE 5a D5969, singled out the Fokker (which he initially identified as a Pfalz) flown by Ltn d R Schultz. Writing in the third person, he reported;

'Lt C H R Lagesse, accompanied by Capt R C L Holme MC and Lt H A Whittaker, saw an enemy Scout over Hazebrouck at about 1800 hrs. All three dived on it. Lt Lagesse fought it to within about 2000 ft of the ground, when it was obviously due to land this side. He then left it, and the enemy aircraft landed north of Hazebrouck and turned over on its nose.'

The Fokker was the fifth of 20 victories for Lagesse.

British authorities were presented with a new and intact D VII on 6 June, when Hans Schultz of *Staffel* Raben was shot down by Lt Lagesse of No 29 Sqn. D VII 386/18 was an early machine from the first Fokker production batch of 300, and is representative of the first examples acquired by *Jasta* 18. This photograph was taken when the fighter was displayed with other captured aircraft in Agricultural Hall in Islington, London. In the background is Fokker Dr I 144/17 of *Jasta* 11, captured with its pilot, Ltn Stapenhorst, on 13 January 1918

The death of such a successful pilot as Mendel, as well as the loss of Schultz as a PoW, must have made it a sobering day for the *Jasta* 18 pilots. In the same combat, Ltn Hebler and Ltn d R Erich Spindler both made SE 5a claims which were not allowed (indeed, No 29 Sqn had no losses). Hans Walter Schultz was another experienced pilot that the *Staffel* could ill afford to lose. Born in Berlin on 27 May 1893, he had joined *Jasta* 15 on 13 November 1917 and earned his pilot's badge on 27 December. After making the big switch with *Jasta* 18 on 20 March, he had achieved his lone confirmed victory on 24 May 1918. He survived his captivity to become a mason and later an architect, and died in Berlin on 20 July 1975.

As Schultz was being led off to captivity, his D VII 386/18 quickly became the object of intense scrutiny by British authorities. It was the first intact example of the type to fall into British hands, and was given the British reference number G/2Brigade/14. Two technical reports on the aircraft survive, revealing that 386/18 had the works number 2455 and Mercedes D IIIa Nr 40957. These reports provide vital, if somewhat contradictory, evidence on the unit colours of *Jasta* 18 at this time. The *Ministry of Munitions Report on Fokker Single-Seater Biplane* had this to say;

'The fabric is coarse flax. It is colour-printed in the usual irregular polygons. The colouring of the machine is interesting. The top surface of the wings is painted a brilliant vermilion, while on the underneath surface the fabric is untouched, and is revealed as the familiar printed colour fabric. The body is red in the front portion – where are the aluminium cowls – except the radiator, which is painted white. From the cockpit to the rear, the colour is white. The vertical surfaces of the tail are also white, and the horizontal surfaces – both top and bottom – black.'

The famous British aeronautical journal *Flight* also published its own evaluation of the D VII, and described its markings in this way;

'As regards the covering of the Fokker biplane, this is chiefly remarkable, in the specimen under review on account of the colours in which it is painted. The front portion of the body and the top portion of the top plane are painted a deep vermilion, while the rear portion of the body is painted white. The lower surfaces of the top plane and the bottom plane are camouflaged in the usual German manner by a printing in different colours of lozenge-shaped figures. The tailplane and elevator are painted black, with the exception of a parallel portion of the top surface, which is painted white like the body.'

Unfortunately, the only known photos of this machine show it after most of its fabric was stripped off for public display at the Agricultural Hall in Islington, London. Fortunately an unknown artist made a detailed sketch of the Fokker before the fabric was removed. The sketch confirms the description in the reports, but also reveals that two black vertical stripes were painted on the aft fuselage. No raven emblem appears in the drawing, and it is likely that the unit insignia had not yet been applied to this D VII when it was shot down. The 'brilliant vermilion' uppersurfaces of the wings and nose, along with the white fuselage aft of the cockpit, formed the conspicuous *Staffel* markings of *Jasta* 18, while the black stripes on the fuselage and black portions of the tailplane were Schultz' personal identification.

Back at the front, meanwhile, changes were in the wind for *Jasta* 18. In the middle of June, the *Staffel* received orders indicating its time with the 6. *Armee* was at an end. The unit was now assigned to the 19. *Armee* and was posted to an airfield at Montingen (Montoy), east of Metz. So the 'Ravens' packed their bags and prepared to wing their way far to the south. Once again, the long and varied history of Royal Prussian *Jagdstaffel* 18 was taking a new and important turn.

The 'Ravens' of *Jasta* 18 flew south to Montingen airfield in June 1918 to oppose the bombers of Britain's Independent Air Force. This group, photographed at Montingen, exudes panache and confidence. From left to right are Glatz, Deberitz, Monnington, Spindler, *Staffelführer* Raben, Baier, Müller, von Büren, Bergner and Schleichardt (*A E Ferko*)

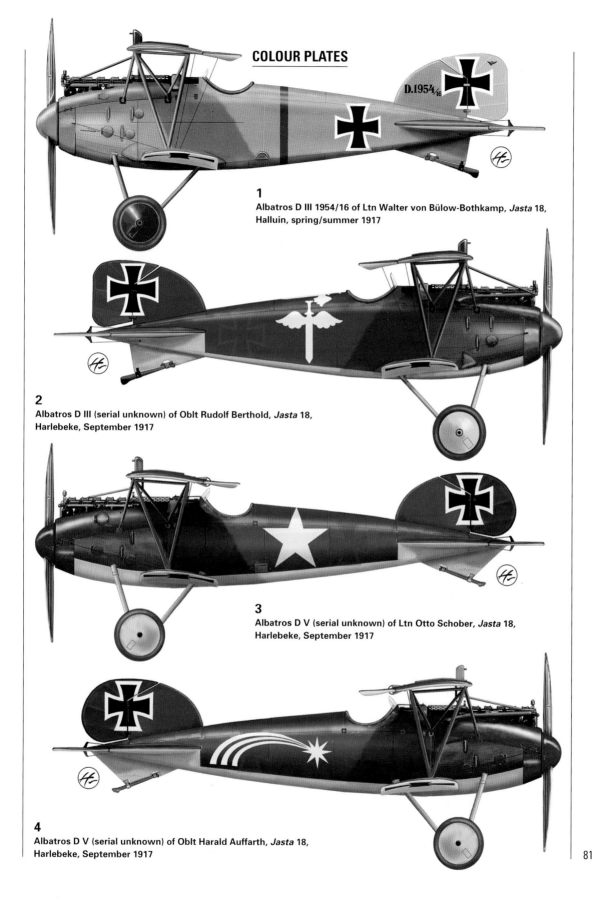

COLOUR PLATES

D.1954/16

1
Albatros D III 1954/16 of Ltn Walter von Bülow-Bothkamp, *Jasta* 18,
Halluin, spring/summer 1917

2
Albatros D III (serial unknown) of Oblt Rudolf Berthold, *Jasta* 18,
Harlebeke, September 1917

3
Albatros D V (serial unknown) of Ltn Otto Schober, *Jasta* 18,
Harlebeke, September 1917

4
Albatros D V (serial unknown) of Oblt Harald Auffarth, *Jasta* 18,
Harlebeke, September 1917

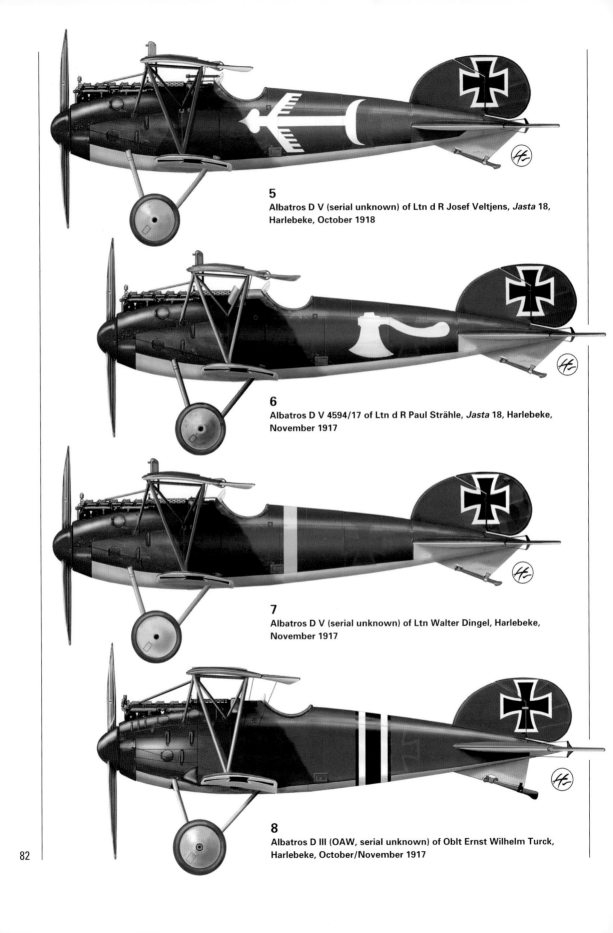

5
Albatros D V (serial unknown) of Ltn d R Josef Veltjens, *Jasta* 18, Harlebeke, October 1918

6
Albatros D V 4594/17 of Ltn d R Paul Strähle, *Jasta* 18, Harlebeke, November 1917

7
Albatros D V (serial unknown) of Ltn Walter Dingel, Harlebeke, November 1917

8
Albatros D III (OAW, serial unknown) of Oblt Ernst Wilhelm Turck, Harlebeke, October/November 1917

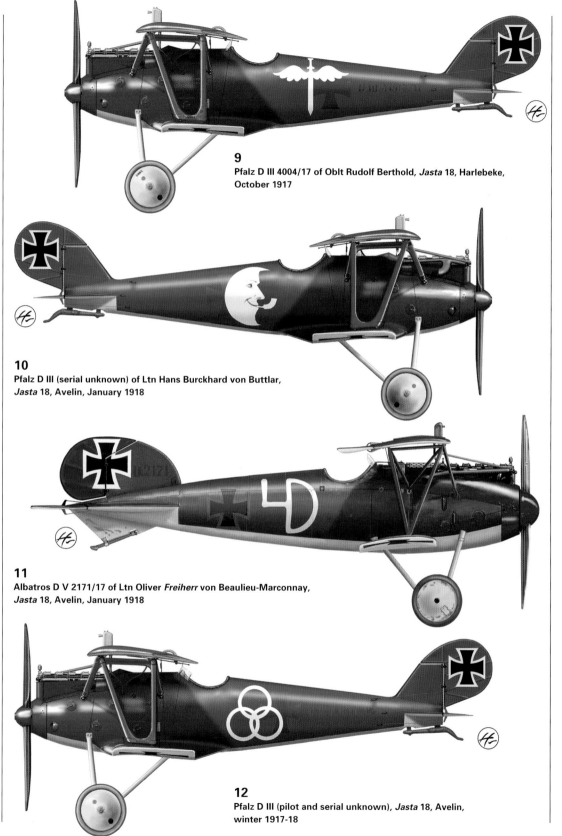

9
Pfalz D III 4004/17 of Oblt Rudolf Berthold, *Jasta* 18, Harlebeke, October 1917

10
Pfalz D III (serial unknown) of Ltn Hans Burckhard von Buttlar, *Jasta* 18, Avelin, January 1918

11
Albatros D V 2171/17 of Ltn Oliver *Freiherr* von Beaulieu-Marconnay, *Jasta* 18, Avelin, January 1918

12
Pfalz D III (pilot and serial unknown), *Jasta* 18, Avelin, winter 1917-18

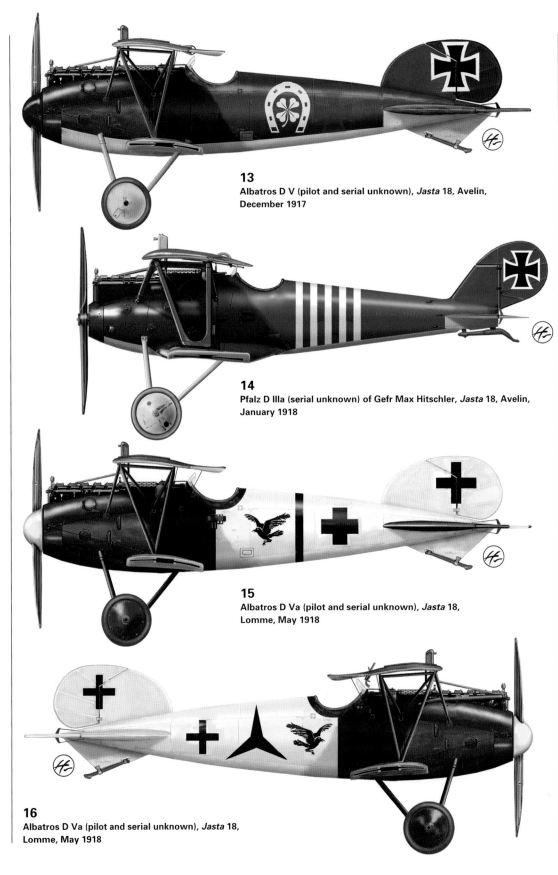

13
Albatros D V (pilot and serial unknown), *Jasta* 18, Avelin,
December 1917

14
Pfalz D IIIa (serial unknown) of Gefr Max Hitschler, *Jasta* 18, Avelin,
January 1918

15
Albatros D Va (pilot and serial unknown), *Jasta* 18,
Lomme, May 1918

16
Albatros D Va (pilot and serial unknown), *Jasta* 18,
Lomme, May 1918

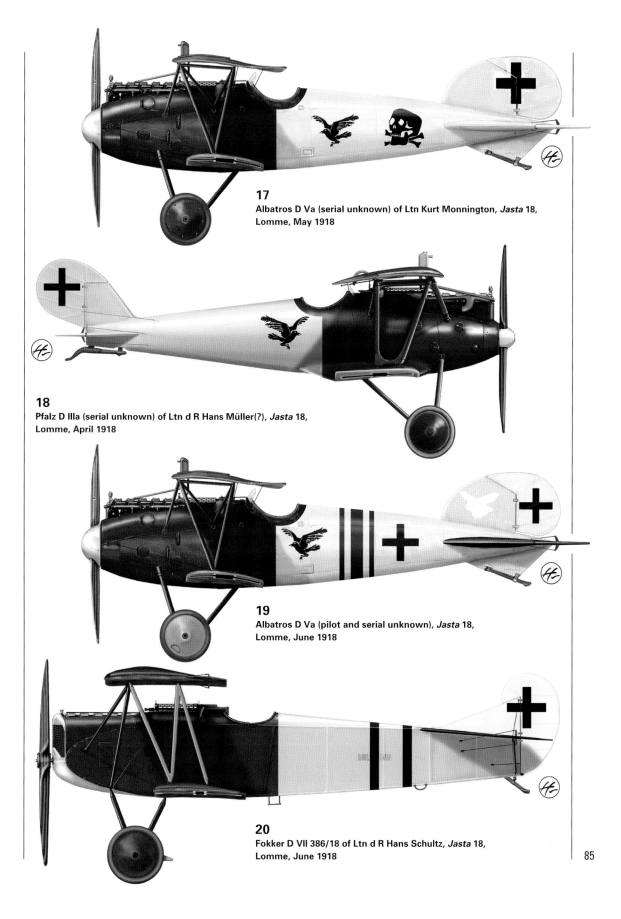

17
Albatros D Va (serial unknown) of Ltn Kurt Monnington, *Jasta* 18,
Lomme, May 1918

18
Pfalz D IIIa (serial unknown) of Ltn d R Hans Müller(?), *Jasta* 18,
Lomme, April 1918

19
Albatros D Va (pilot and serial unknown), *Jasta* 18,
Lomme, June 1918

20
Fokker D VII 386/18 of Ltn d R Hans Schultz, *Jasta* 18,
Lomme, June 1918

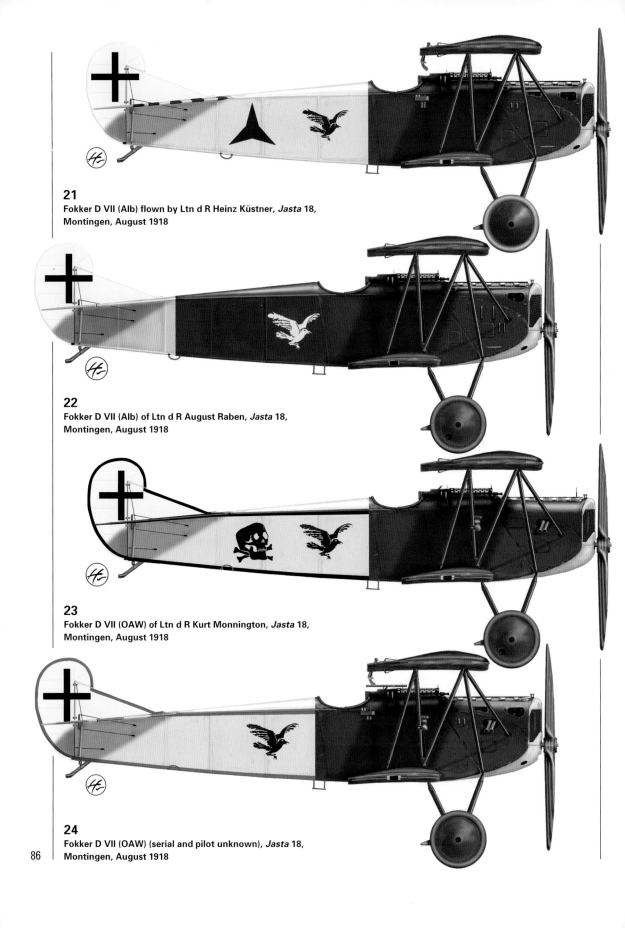

21
Fokker D VII (Alb) flown by Ltn d R Heinz Küstner, *Jasta* 18,
Montingen, August 1918

22
Fokker D VII (Alb) of Ltn d R August Raben, *Jasta* 18,
Montingen, August 1918

23
Fokker D VII (OAW) of Ltn d R Kurt Monnington, *Jasta* 18,
Montingen, August 1918

24
Fokker D VII (OAW) (serial and pilot unknown), *Jasta* 18,
Montingen, August 1918

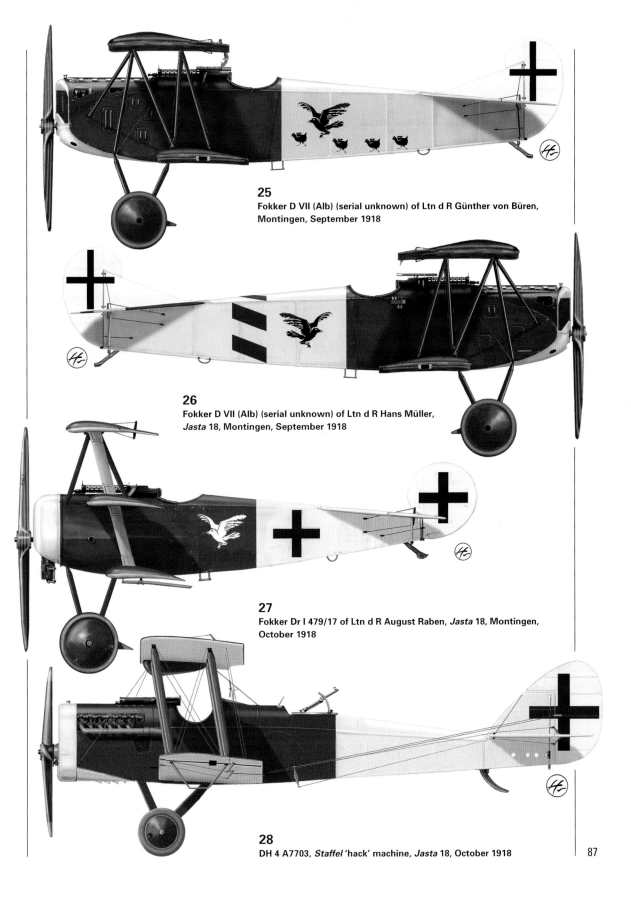

25
Fokker D VII (Alb) (serial unknown) of Ltn d R Günther von Büren,
Montingen, September 1918

26
Fokker D VII (Alb) (serial unknown) of Ltn d R Hans Müller,
Jasta 18, Montingen, September 1918

27
Fokker Dr I 479/17 of Ltn d R August Raben, *Jasta* 18, Montingen,
October 1918

28
DH 4 A7703, *Staffel* 'hack' machine, *Jasta* 18, October 1918

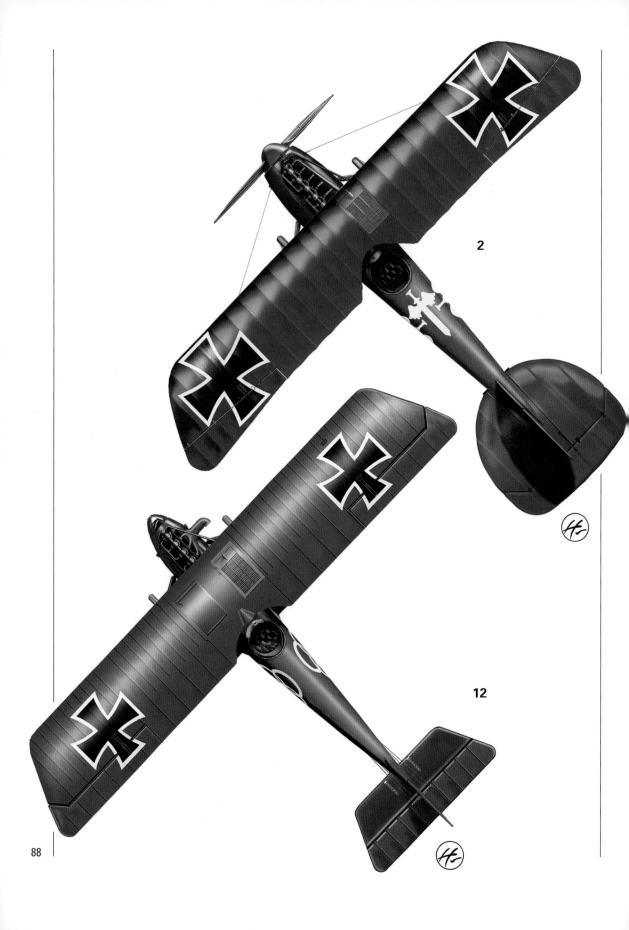

2

12

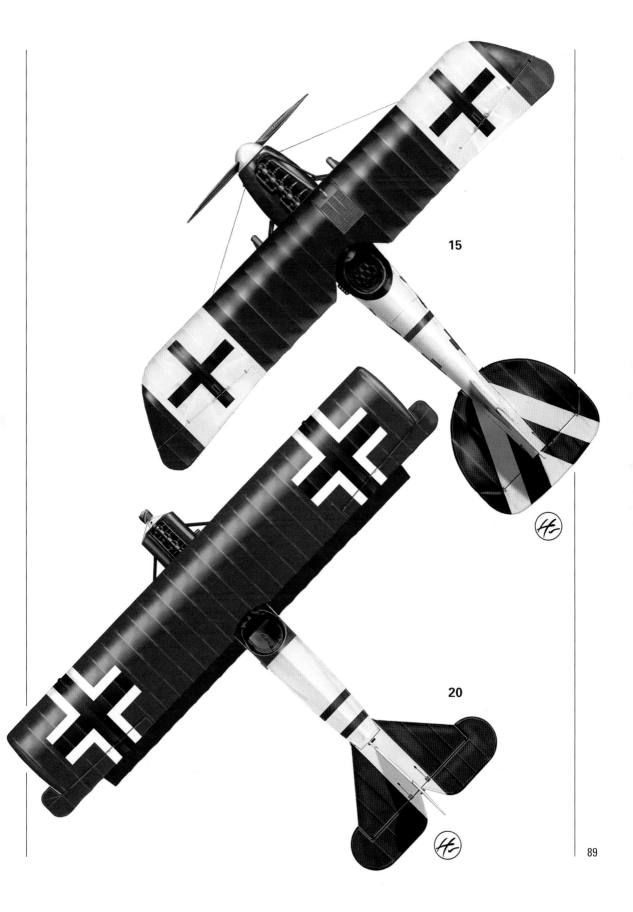

15

20

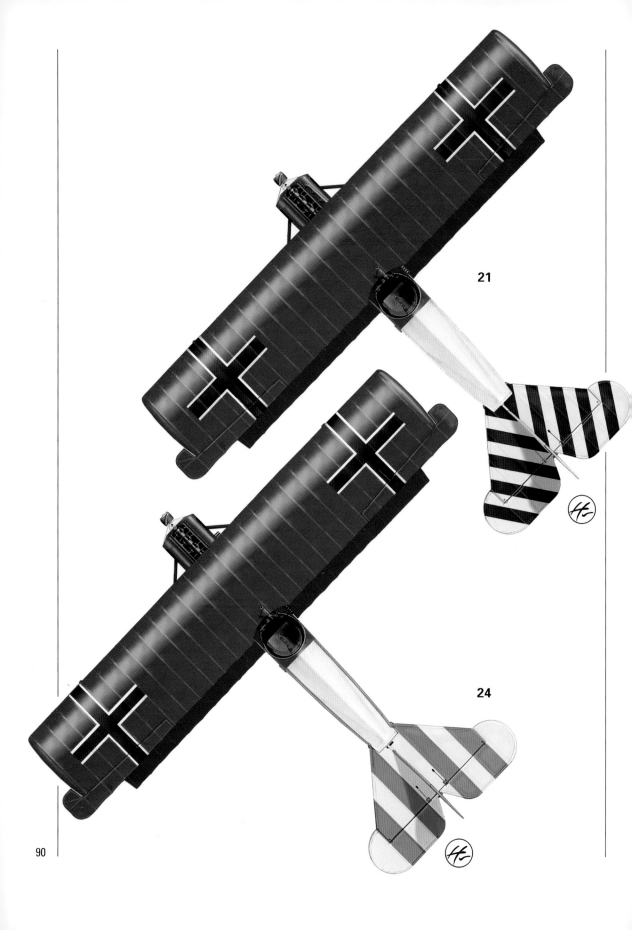

21

24

27

26

THE RAVENS FLY HIGH

The posting of *Jasta* 18 to the 19. *Armee* area of responsibilty came about because of the British bomber offensive against the industrial centres of Germany. More fighters were required to bolster the strength of units attempting to stem the tide of these attacks, which saw bombers flying through the Metz corridor to reach their targets. The campaign had reached a new level of organisation and effort on 6 June 1918 when the Independent Force of the RAF had been formed.

The Independent Force (often known as the IAF, or Independent Air Force) was a strategic bombing formation. It grew out of the RAF's 41st Wing, which had already been carrying out a programme of bomb raids against targets behind the German lines in support of land operations, as well as targets in southwest Germany itself.

Sir William Weir, the Air Minister, appointed Hugh Trenchard as C-in-C of the new IAF, which was made up of two wings of the new VIII Brigade of the RAF. The 41st Wing contained three day bomber squadrons, all based at Azelot aerodrome – No 55 (flying DH 4s) and Nos 99 and 104 (both equipped with DH 9s). The 83rd Wing was composed of two night bombing units. Trenchard explained the objective of the IAF as;

'The breakdown of the German Army in Germany, its government and the crippling of its sources of supply. Railways were first in order of importance as targets, and next in importance the blast furnaces.'

To meet such optimistic objectives the IAF would attempt to raid Germany's coal and iron industry, aerodromes, railways and rolling stock, and manufacturing centres of explosives, aircraft and engines.

In order to meet this growing threat, German defence forces had created an elaborate communications network. It connected observation posts, balloon observers and flak batteries with the aerodromes of the home defence units known as *Kampfeinsitzer Staffeln* (or *KEST*), as well as a few local *Jagdstaffeln* such as 18. Forward observation posts found on high points near the frontlines would keep watch for incoming bomber formations. They were connected by telephone with the 19. *Armee Flakgruko* Headquarters at Frankfurt, which passed the information on the predicted route of the bombers to relevant anti-aircraft batteries. The information was also supplied to *KEST* commanders, as well as the few available *Jasta* airmen, so they could get airborne in an attempt to interdict the IAF formations.

There were nine *KEST* units in existence by this time, and they tended to be equipped with a motley collection of aircraft (some quite outdated) and their pilots were of differing quality as well. Although the commanders were usually ex-*Jasta* pilots with frontline experience, many of the *KEST* pilots were either beginners or worn-out *Jasta* pilots in need of a rest. Thus the *KEST* airmen were hard pressed to deal with the Independent Force's bombing offensive, and *Jasta* 18 was brought in to add its experience and expertise to the defence of southwest

Germany. At the time, the only other *Jagdstaffel* in the 19. *Armee* was *Jasta* 80b at Morsberg.

To the northwest was *Armee Abteilung 'C'* with Württemberg *Jasta* 64 at Mars-la-Tour and *Jasta* 65 at Les Baraques. On the southern flank was *Armee Abteilung 'A'* with *Jasta* 70 and Bavarian 78 at Bühl aerodrome near Saarburg, and *KEST* 3 at Morchingen. These units would perform the lion's share of the interception of IAF formations in this period. *Jasta* 18 was, by far, the most accomplished *Staffel* among them. In the coming days the 'Ravens' would become experts at splitting up the tight formations of bombers so they could pick off the lone strays.

It is believed that the *Staffel* made its move to Montingen on 14 June, although a move of such distance probably took a few days for all the details to be completed. At any rate, the pilots were squared away in comfortable quarters in a large chateau known as *'Schloss* Montingen', and the aircraft were tucked into the long line of low wooden hangars at the airfield. It is likely the unit was fully equipped with D VIIs by this time – along with at least one triplane (Raben's) – but a few Albatros or Pfalz fighters may have still been on strength.

Unfortunately, one of the primary sources on the activities of *Staffel* Raben dries up precisely in this period. According to the late historian A E Ferko, '*Jasta* 18's *Kriegstagebuch* (war diary) ended with 21 June. What became of the remainder of its official written chronology, which was apparently lost or destroyed during the retreat and subsequent return to Germany, remains an enigma'. Thus, the remaining story as related here has been gleaned from the *Nachrichtenblatt* and a variety of other sparse sources, especially the records of the IAF squadrons. It should perhaps be noted here that German pilots in *Jasta* 18 and other units frequently confused the DH 4 and DH 9 in their claims

The vermilion and white Fokker D VIIs of *Staffel* Raben presented a brilliant sight on the ground or in the air. Raben's own D VII (OAW) heads this line-up at Montingen – a mix of both Albatros and OAW-built machines. The machine of the *Staffelführer* was the only one to bear a white raven, with the red colour applied to most of the fuselage (*Küstner*)

and combat reports. Thus, they often claimed one type when in fact they had attacked the other.

BATTLING THE BOMBERS

The first confirmed confrontation between the 'Ravens' of *Jagdstaffel* 18 and the bombers of the IAF took place in the afternoon of 27 June. All three daylight squadrons of the IAF took part in a raid against the railway station, sidings and workshops at Thionville – these combined raids were mounted in the hope of inflicting maximum damage on one lone target. Six aircraft of No 104 Sqn took the lead, with two formations from No 99 Sqn in the rear (each with six DH 9s), while two groups of DH 4s from No 55 Sqn flew above the DH 9s due to their superior engine performance. This massed formation crossed the lines at Pont-à-Mousson and arrived over Thionville at 14,000 ft.

Just after the de Havillands dropped their bombs and turned for home at about 1720 hrs, the fighters of *Jasta* 18 arrived on the scene. Combat reports filed by the British crews described their attackers as two Fokker triplanes and ten Albatros (sic) fighters, all with red wings and white fuselages – it is very likely that the 'Albatros' were misidentified D VIIs (the type still being fairly new to British airmen). The aerial combat was fiercely waged, with the Germans trying to break up the IAF flights.

The leader of the second group of No 99 Sqn's DH 9s, Capt Beecroft, had mistaken the target and taken his formation on a broad turn to make another bomb run. This disorganised his flight and caused it to fall behind the other formations, thus giving the formidable ace Hans Müller exactly the opportunity he was looking for. He slipped into the disoriented group just behind D1669, flown by Lt Chapin (an American) and 2Lt Wiggins. Müller's unerring fire, directed from almost point-blank range, set the DH 9 ablaze. In the lead bomber, Beecroft watched the doomed aircraft in horror and saw the observer

One of the most proficient of the 'Ravens' was Hans Müller, who was the first to score against the bombers of the IAF on 27 June. This rare photograph shows his D VII (Alb), which displayed his usual personal marking of a black and white diagonally striped fuselage band. This same motif was applied to the tailplane in the form of black/white chevron stripes (*J Leckscheid*)

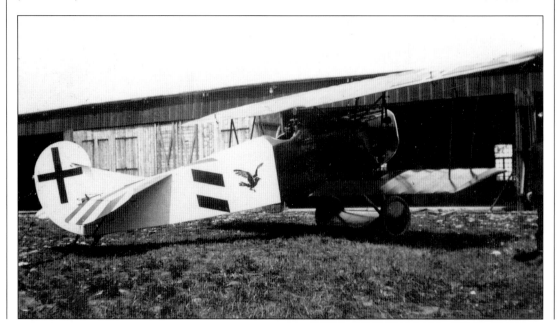

Wiggins climb out of the burning aft cockpit and leap into space near Diedenhofen (Thionville).

Soon after, five of the DH 4 crews from No 55 Sqn bravely turned back and dived down to assist the beleaguered DH 9s. The pilots of *Jasta* 18 pulled away to fight another day, satisfied with Müller's uncontestable sixth victory, which was recorded as an English 'DH 4' (sic), which fell at Kedingen/Lothringen.

Five days later *Staffel* Raben was again in action against the IAF. At 0600 hrs (German time) ten DH 9s took off from No 104 Sqn's field at Azelot, intending to bomb the railways at Karthaus. One of the 'Nines' crashed upon take-off, and engine troubles reduced the formation to just five aircraft soon after it crossed the lines near Verdun. The surviving crews reported that they were attacked by five 'Pfalz' scouts (sic) over Conflans. DH 9 C6307, crewed by pilot Lt McConchie and observer 2Lt Woodman, dropped out of the group, pursued by two of the *Jasta* 18 fighters. Forced down and captured, they were probably the crew of the 'DH 4' credited to Ltn d R Erich Spindler as having been shot down west of Avning for his coveted initial victory.

The DH 9 flight was down to just four machines, so the leader Capt McKay decided to drop their bombs on the secondary target of the triangle of railways at Metz-Sablon. Despite constant pressure from the fighters from *Jasta* 18 (and other units), the four remaining No 104 Sqn crews returned home safely.

On 7 July a new pilot, Ltn Heinz Küstner, arrived at *Jasta* 18. While the pilots of Raben's *Jasta* left behind little or no personal accounts, a brief 'interview' of sorts with Küstner has surfaced. In 1968, the 71-year-old Theodor Rumpel, ace of *Jastas* 16b and 23b, made the acquaintance of Oberst D Küstner, who was then living in Hanau. Rumpel was in touch with American historian William Puglisi, and acquired a statement from Küstner concerning his career as a *Jagdflieger* in the Great War for his friend from the USA. As a rare first-hand account from a pilot

Ltn Heinz Küstner was posted to *Staffel* Raben on 7 July, and he is pictured here at left with Ltn Rodde, the OzbV (adjutant) of the *Jasta*. Küstner's Albatros-built D VII featured a black three-pointed star and reversed chevron stripes on the tail for personal identification. A stencil was used to apply the raven emblem uniformly on every fighter in the unit (*Küstner*)

Küstner's Fokker D VII (Alb) sits in the shade of a hangar at Montingen in a perspective which provides a good view of the stripes on the tailplane and elevators (*Küstner*)

of *Staffel* Raben, Rumpel's brief report on Küstner is worth quoting;

'He joined the squadron on 7 July 1918, which at that time was stationed at Montingen airfield near Metz, France (French name of the airfield is Montoy, the then-German name was Montingen). The leader of *Jasta* 18 was Ltn Raben. The total score of *Jasta* 18 was 126 aerial victories, including a few balloons. Most successful pilot was the leader Ltn Raben (sic), number unknown. The squadron was equipped with Fokker D VII aeroplanes, plus one Fokker triplane flown by Raben. All the aeroplanes were painted red from nose to the cockpit and from there to the tail white. The *Jasta* badge was a black raven, which was painted on the side of the fuselage of each aeroplane.

'*Jasta* 18 was, at the time when he was a member (by which I mean my source of information, Heinz Küstner), attached or subordinated to the Army of Generaloberst Felix Graf von Bothmer (i.e., the 19. *Armee*) and temporarily (in September 1918) to the Army Group of the Crown Prince. On 14 September 1918 *Jasta* 18 scored its 100th victory, reported by the Army's bulletin on 17 September 1918.'

Küstner's statement that the *Jasta* was still equipped with one Fokker Dr I that was generally flown by Raben is interesting, but his recollection that Raben was the 'most successful' pilot in the unit is clearly in error. Raben ended the war with four victories, a score that Müller, Monnington and Kühne would all surpass – but Küstner's forgivable mistake is perhaps a measure of the esteem in which Raben was held by his pilots. Records compiled by modern historians may differ in regard to the precise date of the unit's 100th victory (or its final total), but there is no doubt that at the time it was believed that this milestone was reached on 14 September.

While the men of *Staffel* Raben continued to fly and engage the enemy throughout July, detailed information on their fights is hard to come by. There is an indication that *Jasta* 18 took part in a hard-fought but unsuccessful combat with No 99 Sqn on the afternoon of 22 July. Two flights of six DH 9s had taken off at 1520 hrs in an attempt to bomb the Mercedes Aero Engine Works in the Stuttgart suburb of Untertürkheim, but high winds prevented the long trip to the target and the 12 bombers raided the railway at Offenburg instead.

As the 'Nines' turned for the return trip, their observers swung their Lewis guns into position to deal with some 16 enemy scouts which were approaching. From the available data it seems likely their opponents were a combined force from *Jastas* 18, 78b and 80b.

As the No 99 Sqn machines left their objective the German fighters swept in, diving across the de Havilland formation from left to right. Sgt F L Lee, an observer in DH 9 C6196, reported that some of the

enemy had 'red top planes, with red and white fuselages' – these were certainly from *Jasta* 18. One of the DH 9s was forced down to a safe landing west of the lines. No pilot of *Staffel* Raben achieved a victory this day, but one DH 9 was credited to a *Jasta* 80b pilot while another from *Jasta* 78b made an unconfirmed claim.

Jasta 18 had better luck on 30 July, when it took part in a major interception of eight DH 9s from No 99 Sqn. The bombers hit the railway station at Lahr, and during their long trip homeward they fought a lengthy battle with several formations of German fighters – again from *Jastas* 18, 78b and 80b.

Kurt Monnington closed in on one of the drab-coloured biplanes and fired. He was credited with bringing it down at Rombach for his third victory. This was apparently C6210, flown by Lt G Martin with Lt S G Burton as observer. The DH 9 staggered under a devastating burst from Monnington's D VII that holed its radiator, wounded the pilot in the foot and fatally wounded the observer. Martin managed to crash-land his crippled 'Nine' on the Allied side in a marsh with Burton already dead in the rear cockpit. Another one of the bombers broke up in the air, probably under the fire of a *Jagdflieger* from *Jasta* 78b. However, the steadfast British gunners exacted a measure of retaliation.

Things did not always go *Staffel* Raben's way. On 22 July the *Jasta* participated in a lengthy combat against DH 9s of No 99 Sqn for no gains. It is not known when this OAW-built D VII lost its undercarriage, but this photograph provides details of the additional louvres and cooling holes featured on many *Jasta* 18 Fokkers. The pilot's personal markings included the coloured stripes on the tailplane and borders on the fuselage and fin/rudder (*Küstner*)

Kurt Monnington punished the crews of the IAF throughout the summer of 1918, and would be credited with no less than six of their bombers before war's end. This previously unpublished photograph reveals the markings applied to Monnington's early OAW-built Fokker. This pilot had previously used similar death's head markings on his Albatros fighters in both *Jagdstaffeln* 15 and 18, and an all-black version adorned this Fokker just aft of the raven. The fuselage and all horizontal and vertical tail surfaces received a narrow black border, giving the entire machine a forbidding appearance. Note the outboard position of the cross on the underside of the bottom wing, frequently seen on OAW-built D VIIs

One pilot from Bavarian *Jasta* 78 was wounded and another from *KEST* 4b was killed in combat with the DH 9s.

Jasta 18 was in action against the DH 9s of No 99 Sqn again on the 31st, along with several other *Staffeln* – but with frustrating results. A group of nine de Havillands had managed to make it across the lines, headed for the distant railways at Mainz, but their leader decided to target Saarbrücken instead when German fighters appeared. The bomber crews were attacked by large numbers of enemy scouts on their way to and from the target.

It was a disastrous day for No 99 Sqn as no less than seven of the nine bombers were shot down behind the German lines – nine of the DH 9 crewmen were killed and five were taken prisoner. *Jasta* 18 was amongst their opponents, and Kurt Monnington made a claim for a DH 9 at Grossblittersdorf, south of Saarbrücken. However, it seems his claim was disallowed, as were claims made by pilots from *Jastas* 65, 78b and 80b and *KEST* 2 and 8. The reason these claims went unconfirmed, with seven DH 9s on the ground in the Metz sector as clear-cut evidence, remains unknown. It should be noted that there is some confusion in the sources between Monnington's two consecutive claims on 30 and 31 July. One authority makes no mention of the claim on the 30th and states that Monnington achieved his third confirmed *Luftsieg* on the 31st, but the version related here is believed to be correct.

Having suffered the loss of nine aircraft and crews in just 48 hours, No 99 Sqn was put out of action for a fortnight. On 1 August, however, No 104 Sqn gamely mounted a raid of ten machines against the railway station at Treves, which were intercepted by pilots from *Jagdstaffeln* 18, 67 and 80b. The German fighters attacked just after the bombers left Treves at about 0940 hrs German time. Sgt W Harrop, in DH 9 C2179, and 2Lt P E Appleby, in C6264, both reported firing at 'red' enemy scouts – evidence that *Jasta* 18 was among the opposition. One of the DH 9s was shot down and the crew killed. NCO pilot Wilhelm Kühne of *Staffel* Raben put in a claim for a DH 9, but once again he was unlucky in obtaining confirmation. The claim was instead awarded to Ltn Kurt Seit of *Jasta* 80b. This was the fourth time one of Kühne's claims had failed to be confirmed or been recorded as merely *zur Landung gezwungen.*

One week later on 8 August, far to the northwest in the sectors of the German 18. *Armee* and 2. *Armee,* the British counteroffensive known as the Battle of Amiens opened with a barrage from more than 2000 guns. This was the famous 'Black Day of the German Army' according to Ludendorff, who stated later that on this date he realised the war could no longer be won. The British infantry quickly advanced nine miles and took 16,000 prisoners in less than two hours. After this turning point, German forces all along the front remained on the defensive. In the south in the Metz area, the *Jasta* 18 pilots continued their own defence against the IAF's stubborn bomber offensive.

Although *Jasta* 18's roster of pilots remained remarkably stable for much of the summer of 1918, it is believed that two new pilots were posted in at some point in August. One was Ltn Günther von Büren, who had been born in Berlin-Charlottenburg on 16 October 1895.

These were the 'Ravens'. Few other *Jagdstaffeln* ever exhibited such pride and dash associated with their unit's insignia and colours. The group's 'ready shack' at left was painted in the *Staffel* colours of red and white, and raven emblems were stenciled on as well, apparently in various different hues. From left to right are Glatz, Kühne, Müller, Monnington, Raben, Spindler, Baier, Küstner, Kandt and Schleichardt. Both Monnington and Raben sport what may be captured British 'fug boots' (*Küstner*)

He began the war as a cavalryman in the *königlich sächsischen Ulanen-Regiment* Nr 18. In January 1917 he was flying two-seaters in FA 31, and on the 12th of that month he was awarded the Saxon Albert Order, Knight 2nd Class with Swords. He was destined to down two Allied aircraft and receive an even higher award. The other August arrival was Ltn Kandt, but little is recorded about him.

On 11 August Wilhelm Kühne returned to balloon busting, possibly encouraged by the ease of confirmation that often resulted from the conflagration of a burning 'sausage'. He went after the gasbag of the 7th US Balloon Company near Griscourt (near Dieulouard) and flamed it at about 1630 hrs for his fifth confirmed claim. Observers 1Lt Burt and Sgt Nicholls both parachuted to safety.

Günther von Büren had arrived at the *Staffel* by August, and he is seen here with his groundcrew and dog. He had four running chicks painted on the fuselage to accompany the raven, and these were also probably applied with a stencil. The upper wing crosses appear light-coloured due to the high reflectivity of the black insignia paint (*Küstner*)

Ltn Kandt (sometimes spelled Kant) poses with his groundcrew in front of his OAW-built D VII. The cooling holes in the cowling are clearly seen (*Küstner*)

Another view of Günther von Büren with his Fokker and his perky puppy provides details of his Oigee sight and the cooling holes in the engine cowling

The next day *Staffel* Raben tangled with the DH 9s of No 104 Sqn again. This time, Capt J B Home-Hay led 11 bombers (in two formations) on an early morning raid targeting the Benz Aero Works at Mannheim. Just four miles inside the German lines at Schirmeck, the 'Nines' were intercepted by a large number of enemy scouts, including D VIIs from *Jasta* 18. The pressure from the fighters was severe, but Capt Home-Hay was in an aggressive mood and decided to take the battle to the enemy.

The DH 9s adopted a fighting spread in a semi-circle formation, flying in large circuits, and an intense scrap ensued. Once again, observer Sgt Harrop fired 90 rounds at what he called a 'red Pfalz' and claimed it went down in flames. Home-Hay, at the controls of D7225, dived at a red Fokker that wound up in front of his pilot's gun. He loosed off 50 rounds at 100 yards and watched the D VII go down in left and right hand spins. After 40 minutes of intense combat, all 11 bombers pulled away to bomb their secondary target of the aerodrome at nearby Hagenau.

On the run for home, the rear of the two de Havilland formations was heavily engaged and lost two machines to *Jasta* 18. Kurt Monnington latched on to the tail of DH 9 D2931, flown by 2Lt Meyer and Sgt Wallace. Monnington's accurate Spandau fire holed the bomber's fuel tank, covering Meyer with petrol. Desperate to get his aircraft down before it was engulfed in flames, Meyer landed the intact de Havilland on the aerodrome at Bühl and both British crewmen surrendered. Meanwhile, Richard Schleichardt was attacking DH 9 D3084 piloted by 2Lt Patman. This bomber also had its fuel tank shot up, and the observer, 2Lt McPherson, was wounded in the right arm. The bomber came down safely at Maursmünster and its crew was taken prisoner. These two DH 9s were shot down about 70 miles from *Jasta* 18's base at Montingen, indicating that the tenacious 'Ravens' were ranging far afield in their pursuit of the IAF bombers.

It is likely that the D VIIs flew on an eastward offensive sweep, engaged the DH 9s and then refuelled at Bühl before returning to Metz. At any rate, Monnington had his indisputable fourth *Luftsieg* and Schleichardt his second.

Kurt Monnington was proving to be quite a thorn in side of the IAF, and No 104 Sqn in particular. This Prussian pilot was born on 29 September 1891 in the Altona suburb of Hamburg. He went to war as an NCO in *Grenadier-Regiment* Nr 119 (*Königen Olga*, 1. *Württembergisches*), but soon transferred to another Württemberg unit, *Infanterie-Regiment* Nr 120, in which he was commissioned a leutnant der reserve on 11 November 1914. Monnington received the Iron Cross 2nd Class on 5 June 1915 and the Württemberg Friedrich Order Knight 2nd Class with Swords on 27 November.

On 12 August Monnington scored against No 104 Sqn again when he forced DH 9 D2931 (flown by 2Lt O F Meyer and Sgt A C Wallace) to land at Bühl aerodrome. His fourth victory, this aircraft was one of at least two de Havilland bombers captured intact due to the efforts of *Jasta* 18

Near the end of February 1916 he started pilot training at FEA 4 in Posen. On 27 June his hometown awarded him the Hamburg Hanseatic Cross. The following September Monnington was posted to the home defence unit *KEST* 1 at Mannheim, where he served until briefly posted to *Jasta* 12 on 28 November. For some unknown reason, on 23 January 1917 he was summarily transferred to the relative obscurity of FA(A) 281, a two-seater unit in which he finally received his pilot's badge on 4 May.

He got another chance to prove himself as a *Jagdflieger* on 24 August when he was sent to *Jasta* 22. His assignment there did not last long either, and he wound up in *Jasta* 15 on 6 October. He was, of course, switched to *Jasta* 18 on 20 March, and after scoring his first victory on 11 May he never looked back.

There was no rest for the weary bomber crews of the IAF nor for the fatigued pilots of *Jasta* 18, and 13 August was another day of intense action. Two formations of No 104 Sqn, totalling 12 DH 9s, headed out into a sky filled with patchy clouds on a raid against the Ehrang railway junction. One machine dropped out with engine trouble, and as the formations crossed the frontlines the leader Capt McKay decided to bomb Thionville instead.

Upon their return from the target ten scouts attacked them. The observant No 104 Sqn crews described their assailants as having red wings and white tails and fuselages. Raben's pilots flew into close range and a hot fight ensued – the British observers claimed to have shot down a number of the colourful fighters. In spite of their best efforts, the pilots of the crimson-winged Fokkers could not break up the formations until they reached the frontlines. At this point Monnington picked out a bomber from the second formation, and as he was firing at DH 9 D2281 (crewed by 2Lts Beaufort and Bryant) a flak shell burst directly beneath the bomber. Whether due to the anti-aircraft fire or to Monnington's guns, the DH 9 began to break apart and then collided with DH 9 D7229 in the first formation, flown by 2Lt Leyden and Sgt Windridge. At about 1705 hrs both the de Havillands plunged to earth, locked together, between Arrach and Arnaville. All four crewmen died in the crash.

Fortune smiled on Monnington this day and he was awarded his fifth and sixth victories for these two bombers. The stalwart Wilhelm Kühne also claimed two DH 9s on the 13th. His requests for confirmation were not completely convincing (once again), as his claim for a bomber at Les Eparges was instead awarded to Vzfw Hohly of *Jasta* 65. Apparently Kühne's other supposed victim was awarded to the *Staffelführer* August Raben, who was credited with a 'DH 9' at Altdorf, northeast of Metz, for his third credited *Luftsieg*.

As is usually the case the fog of war makes identifying these aircraft problematic, a difficulty further compounded by the confusion between DH 4s and DH 9s. These machines may well have come from Nos 205 and 206 Sqns. No 205 Sqn lost one DH 4 crew killed on a photo-reconnaissance mission and had another aircraft shot up on a raid to Péronne. One DH 9 crew of No 206 Sqn was killed on an afternoon mission and the observer in another aeroplane was fatally wounded.

August Raben despatched his third credited adversary on 13 August. Here, the *Jastaführer* is seen being assisted by his mechanics as he prepares for a flight – note the crash helmet and parachute harness. The red uppersurface of the top wing is particularly evident (*Küstner*)

For the next fortnight, *Jasta* 18 did not achieve any further victories against the bombers of the IAF. On 28 August, however, Wilhelm Kühne achieved a 'double', and this time both victories were confirmed. At about 1230 hrs he attacked a balloon of the US 6th Balloon Company at Demevre-en-Haye, northwest of Trembelcourt, and succeeded in flaming it – the observer, 1Lt Nixon, parachuted successfully. According to American observers on the ground, the aircraft that attacked their balloon was a Fokker triplane. If so, perhaps Kühne borrowed Raben's Dr I for this mission – or just possibly *Jasta* 18 had a couple of triplanes? The defensive gunners of the 6th Balloon Company also claimed to have damaged the attacking Fokker so badly that it made a forced landing behind the German lines.

As previously noted, pets were a ubiquitous part of life in most *Jagdstaffeln*, and *Staffel* Raben certainly had its share. Besides the five dogs of various breed and size, both a fox and a small porcine creature appear in this photograph. From left to right in the front row are Monnington, Raben, Bergner and Schleichardt. In the rear, again from left to right, are Spindler, Deberitz (standing), Müller, Baier and Glatz (*Küstner*)

Here, *Staffelführer* Raben, wearing his favourite fur-trimmed flight jacket, uses a stepladder to climb into his D VII. The greater display of the vermilion colour on the fuselage facilitated easy identification of the commander's machine in the air (*Küstner*)

Staffelführer Raben's Fokker Dr I turned up in French hands after the war. The commander's white raven emblem was also applied to this machine. The original square white fields for the crosses on the upper wing were thinly overpainted in red, and full-chord *Balkenkreuz* insignia were applied. According to Alex Imrie, the serial number of this machine was 479/17 (*A E Ferko*)

Despite this claim, German records state that at 1235 hrs Kühne successfully sent a two-seater down trailing smoke at Trembelcourt for his seventh *Luftsieg*. Although Kühne described this as a DH 4, it may in fact have been an American Salmson 2A2 of the 12th Aero Squadron, which nonetheless escaped unharmed.

Readers may wonder why August Raben retained a Dr I for his personal use, as well as his D VII, at this late period of the war when the biplane Fokker was a greatly superior aeroplane. According to the respected *Jasta* historian A E Ferko, 'Raben was said to have a fondness for the nimble little Dreidecker and apparently kept it to the end' – something that a few other successful aces did as well. *Jasta* 3 pilot Franz Bacher told Ferko that he kept a Dr I on hand for use when the cloud base was low, whereupon he could exploit the Triplane's unmatched agility. Otherwise, he flew his D VII. In the words of Alex Imrie, 'Some pilots preferred the triplane for low-altitude work, where its manoeuvrability was better than that of the D VII, and it was used, for example, in attacks against observation balloons'.

A less familiar view of Raben's Dr I in French hands after the war reveals the white cowling. It has long been assumed that the interplane struts were red, but this view indicates they were factory finish light blue. It is difficult to determine if the wing undersides were also light blue, or overpainted red (*C Cony*)

Staffelführer Raben poses with DH 4 7703, which he forced down on 30 August for his fourth and final triumph. The No 55 Sqn crew of 2Lts Doehler and Papworth were captured. This DH 4 was taken over as a unit 'hack' by *Jasta* 18 and repainted in the squadron's red and white colours, including the wing uppersurfaces (*Küstner*)

Jasta 18 resumed its feud with the IAF on the 30th – a day of triumph and tragedy for the men of the *Staffel*. Led by Ltn Raben, they took off from Montingen in the morning to intercept a formation of DH 4s from No 55 Sqn headed for the railway sidings at Thionville.

The group of six DH 4s had become separated from a following formation of six other machines, and over Bouley they were first attacked by 'Pfalz' scouts (probably from *Jasta* 65) and then by 'red' Fokkers from *Staffel* Raben. One of the DH 4s, hit by flak, dropped out of formation and was quickly set upon by 'four Fokker D VIIs, two Triplanes and two Pfalz'. The de Havilland was badly riddled and the pilot, Lt Tanney, was wounded twice in the chest. Struggling to remain conscious, he managed to put his machine down behind enemy lines. The victorious German pilot landed nearby and helped the observer, 2Lt Gormley, lift the unconscious pilot from the front cockpit. Both IAF crewmen survived as PoWs.

After the other five DH 4s had dropped their ordnance, the *Jasta* fighters attacked even more tenaciously. British observer 2Lt Gompertz described the scouts as 'single-seaters, either Fokker D VII or Albatros, who dived in everywhere'. Gompertz ran out of ammunition and was lightly wounded in the running battle, but his pilot succeeded in crash-landing within his own lines, despite having the left aileron controls shot away.

What had once been a tight formation of bombers was now completely broken up by the persistent Fokkers, and Ltn Raben latched onto DH 4 7703 marked with a white 'K' on its nose. He succeeded in forcing the crew of pilot 2Lt Doehler and observer 2Lt Papworth down to a landing two kilometres south of Amanweiler at 1200 hrs for his fourth and ultimate victory, and his victims were lucky to survive as prisoners. The crews of two other 'Fours' were not so fortunate, 2Lts Laing and Myring being killed in German territory, while the wounded crew of 2Lts Cunningham and Quinton somehow made it back across the lines to crash near Toul – both men later died.

Only one of the six DH 4s in the first formation from No 55 Sqn landed untouched at Azelot. *Jasta* 18's Günther von Büren was credited

with a DH 4 at Ennerchen for his first victory. However, the DH 4 gunners had put up a valiant defence and the *Jagdstaffel* pilots did not escape unscathed from this day's action. At some point in the far-ranging combat, Ltn Raben found himself in a bad situation under the fire of several British machines. Wilhelm Kühne, the persistent NCO pilot, saw his *Staffelführer* in peril and rushed in to his aid. He is credited with saving his commander's life, but Kühne was in turn shot down and killed by the stubborn fire of No 55 Sqn's crews.

The loss of Offz Stv Kühne was a bitter blow for *Jasta* 18 and a sorry trade for the two DH 4s credited to the unit. Kühne had always been in the thick of every combat, and was a determined and unrelenting air fighter, the unit's resident 'balloon buster'. During his long career he had put in a total of 13 claims, but too often the fortunes of war failed him and only seven were confirmed (four of them being balloons). His was another irreplaceable loss for the *Staffel*.

The 22-year-old nobleman Günther von Büren would, in contrast, survive the war and receive a singular honour for his first victory. On 24 October he was awarded Saxony's highest decoration for bravery, the Knight's Cross of the Military St Henry Order (*Militär St Heinrich Orden*). His citation read, 'Ltn von Büren played a distinguished role in the tough air battles of 1918 and was an exemplary model himself. On 30 August 1918, Ltn von Büren shot down a British aircraft from among an enemy squadron near Arnaville, south of Metz'.

The month of September brought no respite to Germany's weary *Jagdflieger*, including those of *Jasta* 18. The pressure from the Allied aerial forces steadily increased, even as the *Luftstreitkräfte* struggled with shortages of fuel, oil and other resources. The pilots of *Staffel* Raben failed to post a single victory for a fortnight following Kühne's death, although they continued engaging the IAF. The *Jasta* was certainly in combat, though unsuccessful, on 7 September.

On that date Nos 99 and 104 Sqns mounted a combined raid on the Badische Anilin Soda Fabrik Works, a large chemical factory located on

Wilhelm Kühne was killed in combat with No 55 Sqn's DH 4s on 30 August. He is seen here, second from right, in the summer of 1918 with *Jasta* 18 groundcrew and what is believed to be his D VII at Montingen. The fighter was marked with a 'slotted' diagonal black band on the rear fuselage and coloured tailplane/elevators as personal markings. However, Kühne died in a differently marked Fokker (perhaps a borrowed machine), while an aircraft marked very much like this one survived the war (*Küstner*)

Staffelführer Raben is in the centre of this group, wearing British 'fug' boots and with his back to the camera. A lively discussion is taking place during a pre-flight briefing. On the shed in the background is an enemy aircraft recognition chart (*Küstner*)

the Rhine at Ludwigshafen, near Mannheim. The British formations, totalling 12 DH 9s from No 99 Sqn and ten from No 104 Sqn, were first attacked by German fighters on their outward route near Saverne. One DH 9 from No 99 Sqn was shot down before the formations dropped their bombs, and the rest were heavily engaged on the return trip and suffered heavy casualties. By the time they neared the frontlines they were down to 7000 ft, and the trailing crews of No 104 Sqn found themselves locked in combat with six D VIIs with 'scarlet wings and white fuselages'. The *Jasta* 18 pilots failed to bring down any of the DH 9s, but it had still been a disastrous day for No 104 Sqn, which lost seven crewmen killed, wounded or captured. The victories went to pilots from *Jastas* 3 and 80b, as well as *KEST* 1a.

THE BATTLE OF ST MIHIEL

Raben's pilots were soon to face different foes due to the American effort to take the St Mihiel salient in *Armee Abteilung 'C'*, which bordered the sector of the 19. *Armee* on the northwest. For several weeks French and US commands had been planning an offensive to reduce the salient, which had been a wedge-shaped bulge in the French lines south of Verdun since 1914. Gen John J Pershing, overall commander of the American Expeditionary Force, was determined that this would be the first test of a US army under its own commanders.

For the assault scheduled for 12 September, Pershing had assembled a massive force on the flanks of the salient that included 19 divisions totalling 665,000 men, approximately 3000 artillery pieces and 267 tanks. To support this effort the commander of the First Army Air Service, Brig Gen William Mitchell, had built up a huge multinational air armada totalling some 1481 aircraft – at least on paper.

The majority of Mitchell's force was made up of French and American squadrons, aided by three Italian Caproni bomber units and the voluntary assistance of Trenchard's IAF. The German fighter elements opposing this vast force were composed of several mediocre

Jagdstaffeln and the four crack *Staffeln* of JG II, the latter unit having just moved to the sector a few days before. To add muscle to the German opposition the *Jasta* 18 pilots would fly patrols into the sector of the neighbouring *Armee Abteilung 'C'*.

The Germans were only partially surprised when the offensive broke on 12 September. In anticipation of the attack, plans had already been made to evacuate the salient and take up positions in the so-called *Michelstellung*, and in fact the evacuation was already underway. On the first day of the battle heavy rain, low clouds and strong winds hampered aerial activity, yet the elite pilots of JG II downed nine aircraft. This had little effect on the ground battle, however, as the American infantry advanced swiftly on both flanks of the salient.

By the battle's second day – Friday the 13th – nearly all of the American objectives had been reached and the salient had been reduced. However, aerial combat continued over the battle area for several more days. *Jasta* 18 logged its first victory on this front on the 13th as Hans Müller claimed an 'English DH 4' west of Thiaucourt at 0910 hrs for his seventh confirmed opponent. His victim is difficult to identify with certainty, but it may have been an American Liberty-engined DH 4 from the American 8th Aero Squadron. The unit lost one crew killed in action against a group of D VIIs.

On 14 September broken clouds allowed the sun to appear for the first time since the campaign began. A high ceiling allowed for a great deal of aerial combat, resulting in a legendary fight between the 'Ravens' and SPAD XIIIs of the 13th Aero Squadron (bearing a 'grim reaper' unit insignia).

That morning Capt Charles J Biddle, commander of the 13th, led all three flights – 14 SPADs in all – on a patrol 'between the large three-fingered lake, northwest of Thiaucourt, and the east bank of the Moselle River'. A veteran of *escadrille* SPA73 and the 103rd Aero Squadron,

Staffel Raben airmen please the photographer with a quick gathering. Seated in front, from left to right, are Küstner, Monnington and unknown. Standing, again from left to right, are Bergner, Rodde (OzbV), Spindler, unknown, unknown, Glatz, Müller, unknown, Kandt and Baier (*Küstner*)

with five victories, Biddle was one of the best squadron leaders in the USAS, but most of his eager pilots were very green. The unit had been ordered to stay low (below 3500 metres), as another squadron was on patrol at a greater altitude. Unbeknownst to Biddle, the 'Yanks' were being stalked by a *Kette* of D VIIs from *Jasta* 18 above them. The *Kette* was outnumbered (the Americans variously reported only three or four Fokkers), but included the redoubtable Hans Müller as well as Günther von Büren and Heinz Küstner. Undaunted by their opponents' numbers, at 0900 hrs (0800 hrs Allied time) the pilots of the scarlet and white Fokkers struck, diving on the first flight.

1Lt Leighton Brewer, one of the SPAD pilots, recalled the events of this tragic day in 1961;

'We were given a low patrol – 2500 metres – and we were flying this when we were attacked by a bunch of red-nosed Fokkers. We lost four aeroplanes within one minute! I was flying between a couple of men who were shot down, but I only got one bullet in the tail of my aeroplane. The first indication that I had of the thing was seeing a red Fokker with a white fuselage standing on its nose and spraying the fellow in back of me with bullets. Two Fokkers with red wings and noses, and white fuselages, came down on us and they shot down the men on either side of me.'

Heinz Küstner strikes a classic *Jagdflieger* pose in front of his D VII (Alb) at Montingen. He wears one of the coveted British leather flying coats. The rack for flare cartridges and a flare pistol affixed to the upper wing centre section were standard accessories in *Jasta* 18 (*Küstner*)

Jasta 18 pilots, especially Hans Müller, had a great day flying against the American 13th Aero Squadron on 14 September. The captured and repainted DH 4 7703 forms the backdrop for this group at Montingen. Seen from left to right are Kandt, Kurt Monnington (with canine friends), Müller, Raben, Baier and Küstner (*Küstner*)

Besides this account, Brewer also penned *Riders of the Sky* in 1934, a fictionalised but accurate epic poem based on his experiences in the 13th Aero Squadron. Of the first moments in this fight, he wrote of his fictional alter ego, 'A scarlet Fokker with a tail of white and small black crosses on the wing came through them like a comet, and he saw two streams of silver-feathered arrows stab the aeroplane behind him'.

The first 13th Aero Squadron pilot to fall – most likely to Müller's deadly fire – was 1Lt George Kull, killed in SPAD 4562 (with squadron number '11' on the fuselage) that Brewer saw 'go down smoking considerably'. The second was probably 1Lt A A 'Steve' Brody in SPAD 15145 (No '12'), who was lucky to survive as a PoW. Brody's SPAD was later brought to the *Jasta* 18 aerodrome at Montingen as a trophy. Biddle's combat report stated;

'Three Fokkers dove on the rear of the patrol from above, opening fire on Lt J J Seerley. Lts Guthrie and Stiles attacked one, firing several

1Lt Alton A 'Steve' Brody of the 13th Aero Squadron was one of the luckier victims of *Jasta* 18 on the disastrous third day of the St Mihiel offensive. He was captured unhurt, and his intact SPAD XIII 15145 No '12' was brought to the airfield at Montingen as yet another trophy. He is pictured here with a SPAD of the 22nd Aero Squadron (*A D Toelle*)

hundred rounds at short range. Those Fokkers attacked by the 13th had red wings and tails. They also had red bodies as far as the pilot's seat. The rest of the fuselage was pure white. Black crosses on wings and tail.'

1Lts R M Stiles and M K Guthrie submitted this report;

'A biplane Fokker dove on the rear of Flight 1. Lts Guthrie from Flight 2 and Stiles from Flight 1 at once dove on this aeroplane, opening fire at 100 metres and closing to 20 metres. Both pilots saw their tracers entering the fuselage of the Fokker, which was last seen at 2000 metres going straight down in a nose dive. We're not positive whether the Fokker was in or out of control. The Fokker had red wings and a red fuselage forward of the pilot's seat, and a red vertical stabiliser.'

1Lt G D Stivers also claimed to have downed one of the gaudy Fokkers after he fired 'about 150 rounds. I am sure that the fire took effect and the enemy aeroplane disappeared from sight in the region of Pagny-sur-Moselle. I noticed three other Fokkers in the combat painted the same (red fuselage and white tail)'. Although Stiles, Guthrie and Stivers would be credited with two Fokkers, the only *Jasta* 18 casualty was Ltn von Büren, who claimed a SPAD for his second victory before he was wounded in the combat.

Flying SPAD 4486 (No '4'), 1Lt H B Freeman saw another SPAD being pursued by a single Fokker. He dived steeply to assist his comrade and wound up flying eight kilometres behind the German lines. At that point Freeman's motor failed and he was forced to land on the east bank of the Moselle, where he was taken prisoner.

Meanwhile, Hans Müller almost certainly went on to shoot down 1Lt Charles W Drew in SPAD 4578 (No '5'), who suffered through a harrowing ordeal. Drew had dropped out of his place in the first flight due to a failed magneto, but struggled to keep up with the squadron. He then witnessed three D VIIs 'dive through our first flight, partially breaking up the formation. Two of our aeroplanes went down with the last Fokker. They were apparently in trouble, so I dove from my position then at the right rear of the formation, and at an altitude of 2000 metres engaged the enemy aeroplane nose on at a range of about 150 metres, receiving an incendiary bullet in my right thigh, partially paralysing my right leg. I continued the fight, although greatly handicapped by my loss in speed and inability to use my right leg.

'While *viraging* for position I received several direct bursts, one bullet ripping my blouse open and another my breeches. Finally, at about 0910 hrs, I was hit in the right arm by an explosive bullet. The shock twisted my body in the straps and I fainted while trying to grasp the control stick with my left hand. The aeroplane fell out of control for a distance of about 1500 metres, and the rush of air partially revived me. My only recollection of landing was a flash of green in front of me

SPAD XIII 15145 No '12' of the 13th Aero Squadron wound up as a trophy on the *Jasta* 18 airfield at Montingen. It had been flown by 1Lt 'Steve' Brody, who was taken PoW on 14 September 1918. The squadron's Grim Reaper insignia apparently had not yet been painted onto this aircraft, although others downed that day did bear the emblem (*A D Toelle*)

1Lt Charles W Drew suffered terrible injuries when he was downed on 14 September, most likely by Hans Müller. Shot in the right arm and leg by incendiary bullets, he would survive the amputation of his right arm and live for many more years (*A D Toelle*)

and pulling back on the control lever. I struck the ground hard, crushing my landing gear and lower wings, but I didn't receive any further personal injuries, however.

'The fight began southwest of Metz and I was brought down some distance south of the Frescaty aerodrome. The enemy aeroplane was painted a brilliant scarlet on the upper and lower wings, engine housing and three-quarters of the way back on fuselage, while the tail sections were striped black and white. My motor housing was smoking and the aeroplane was riddled by machine gun fire. I managed to unbuckle my strap and get out, my right leg and arm being paralysed. I only crawled a few feet in the direction of a wood when I again fainted.'

Drew's wounds were treated by a German infantry captain, who put tourniquets on both his right arm and leg. During interrogation by an intelligence officer, he was told of the fate of the others in his flight – Lt Freeman and Lt Brody were PoWs and Lt Kull had been killed. The officer knew they were all from the 13th Aero Squadron of the 2nd Pursuit Group. Incredibly, Drew survived a series of operations and the amputation of his right arm in captivity.

After the *Kette* of Fokkers landed back at Montingen and the combat reports were submitted, confirmation of the following claims was obtained. Müller was credited with a SPAD near Gorz (Gorze) at 0900 hrs for his eighth victory and von Büren claimed one at the same location five minutes later for his second. Another SPAD was brought down by Müller at 1910 hrs southwest of Sillningen, then Müller's third of the day fell near Göhn (Goin), southeast of Metz, at 0915 hrs. According to one source, Heinz Küstner was also credited with a SPAD near Thiacourt at 0915 hrs for his first accredited *Luftsieg*.

Hans Müller had experienced an incredible morning, but he was not through for the day. During a later patrol at 1440 hrs, he once again attacked some SPADs and destroyed one west of Pont-à-Mousson. This was possibly SPAD VII 5905 from *escadrille* SPA153, its pilot, Maréchal-des-Logis Pierre de Villeneuve, being killed. It should be

1Lt Brody's SPAD XIII is seen on the left of this view of Montingen airfield, with the captured DH 4 7703 on the right in full *Staffel* colours (*Küstner*)

pointed out that on a brief list of his victories compiled by Müller after the war, the fourth SPAD of the day is listed only as *zur Landung gezwungen,* but it is fully confirmed in most sources. Four in one day was a brilliant accomplishment for Müller, and one matched by only a handful of other German aces of the Great War. According to Küstner, one of the successes achieved this day counted as the 100th confirmed claim of *Jasta* 18. There obviously must have been an incredible celebration at *Schloss* Montingen that evening.

As unlikely as it seems, it is possible that a different *Kette* of Fokkers from *Staffel* Raben was also aloft that eventful morning of the 14th and had a run-in with another American ace. Capt Edward V Rickenbacker of the 94th Aero Squadron was on a voluntary lone patrol and was returning from the lines at 4000 metres at about 0810 hrs when he saw a diamond formation of four D VIIs. His combat report stated;

'Met four enemy Fokkers, with red wings, light grey fuselages and striped tails, over the towns of Villicey and Waville. They were flying at about 3000 metres. I *piqued* (dived) on the upper man of the formation, fired approximately 200 rounds and saw him go down, apparently out of control. Was unable to follow him on account of the other three, who showed excellent fighting spirits.'

Rickenbacker's book *Fighting the Flying Circus* provides a more vivid account;

'No sooner did my guns begin to crackle than the leader of the flight swung up his machine in a climbing *virage,* the other two pilots immediately following his example. Now, as these three light Fokkers began simultaneously to come about at me, I found myself staring full into three beautiful scarlet noses headed straight in my direction. It scarcely needed their colour to tell me who they were, for the skill with which they all came about so suddenly convinced me that this was no place for me. I had blundered single-handedly into the von Richthofen crowd (sic). No matter where I turned there were always at least two of them there before me! I need no more proof of the flying ability of the

The details of this D VII crash are unknown, but the aircraft was marked with a coloured tailplane and broad vertical fuselage band as personal insignia. The rare view of the underside of the wings proves that this surface was *not* invariably painted red as some have supposed, but remained in printed 'lozenge' fabric

celebrated German squadron of fighting pilots. They whipped their machines about me with incredible cleverness.'

Rickenbacker used his SPAD's speed and superior diving ability to escape his opponents, and would be credited with his seventh of 26 victories from this encounter. Although the 'Yank' ace was certain he had encountered 'Richthofen's Circus' his description of red wings and noses, 'light grey' fuselages and striped tails leads this author to believe these were *Jasta* 18 Fokkers.

Sunday, 15 September brought the end of the St Mihiel campaign. Both American airmen and German *Jagdflieger* were active over the front in spite of the low clouds and rainy skies. *Staffel* Raben was out in force that morning and ironically encountered the 'Grim Reapers' of the 13th Aero Squadron again, but with inconclusive results. A patrol of ten SPADs, led by 1Lt Stovall, was at 5200 metres over Vaux at 1010 hrs when they spotted nine red-winged *Jasta* 18 D VIIs and one brown Fokker from another *Jasta*, acting as a decoy, slightly below them. Recognising their opponents of the previous day, the 13th Aero Squadron pilots were out for retaliation. Brewer later recalled;

'The next day [the 15th] Hank Stovall led a group of us and we caught this "Circus" climbing up and we got three of them (sic). I remember seeing a Fokker, with Stovall's SPAD right behind him, so I tipped up and sprayed in front of him so he had to go through my fire as well as Stovall's. The Fokkers all had red noses and wings, but some seemed to have white fuselages, and others had grey.'

1Lt M K Guthrie reported;

'Saw one biplane Fokker painted brown at about 1010 hrs over Vaux. Leader attacked and I followed, firing three bursts of about 15 shots each. Looking up, I saw a formation of about nine Fokkers with red fuselage front ends and wings and white tails. Pulled up to gain altitude and attack with rest of patrol.'

The 13th Aero Squadron pilots were satisfied that they had gained the upper hand in this fight, and three red-nosed D VIIs were confirmed to them – but *Jasta* 18 had no casualties or victories this day.

Leighton Brewer also included this combat in *Riders in the Sky*, in which he described the Fokker pilots as 'the Flying Circus – Richthofen's war-hawks' (sic). His fictional protagonist marvelled at the D VII's famous ability to 'hang on its prop'. He saw;

'That Fokker red and white, the one who yesterday had nicked George Kull. The Boche ace rose up on his red right wing in a climbing turn such as he never dreamed could be. It seemed as if that Fokker just stood on its tail. The Spandaus barked a short burst.'

Like Brewer, Charles Biddle had great respect for the formidable enemies who flew the colourful Fokkers. In a letter written on 14 October, Biddle described one such opponent;

Jasta 18 pilots encountered American airmen again on 15 and 16 September but failed to achieve any more successes. After the war, a number of Fokkers from *Staffel* Raben came into 'Yank' hands and were the objects of great interest. One of them was this D VII (Alb) that was identified by a black chevron on the fuselage and a black(?) tailplane with a white chevron. Sadly, the pilot of this machine is unknown

'He was one of the most gaudily painted boys you ever laid eyes on, with bright red wings and fuselage as far back as the pilot's seat, and the rest of the body pure white with black crosses. The pilots are certainly good, there is no use denying that fact. They have lots of fight in them and the way some of them can throw their machines around in the air shows you clearly that they are old hands at the game. I would like to drop one of that red-winged outfit. We knocked a couple of them down in the last offensive, but they got more of us than we did of them.'

On 16 September the *Jasta* 18 pilots were back to stalking DH 4 bombers, but this time they were American-built aeroplanes from the 20th Aero Squadron of the US 1st Day Bombardment Group. During the mopping up operations of the St Mihiel battle, the DH 4s left Amanty aerodrome at 1245 hrs to bomb the railway yards at Conflans. 1Lt William Stull Holt was an observer on that raid, and he penned this account in a letter;

'There were five aeroplanes that went over together and we bombed a railway yard with pretty fair results. The anti-aircraft fire was pretty heavy. I counted more than 100 bursts in the air at once, and more were coming up all the time. Some Boche aeroplanes came up after us, eight of them with wings painted bright red and with white bodies. They ran into most of their own "archies"' (flak) fire, which came a lot nearer them than us, a thing which tickled us all. They weren't able to catch us, not even getting within gunshot – at least no one fired at all. So they withdrew and we went peaceably homeward.'

An official report describing this raid stated, 'Seven enemy aircraft reported as biplane Fokkers with rose coloured wings and white fuselages followed the flight of the 20th from Brainville to Chambley at 1410 hrs.'

Oddly enough, some pilots of *Jasta* 18 may have been active elsewhere on the 16th. Hans Müller's privately compiled listing of his own victories states that he downed what he called a 'SPAD two-seater' for his 11th *Luftsieg* on 16 September at a location recorded as 'Hayingen'. However, this victory is not included in any of the recent compilations made from more accessible historical sources. It is another example of

Towards the end of the war, cooler temperatures are evident as six officers satisfy the photographer with *Jasta* commander Ltn d R August Raben. From left to right are two unknowns, then Ltn Bergner, Ltn Rodde (OzbV), Raben, Ltn Heinz Küstner and another unknown (who wears an observer's badge). Many years later, Küstner would claim that *Jasta* 18 was credited with 126 confirmed victories. Raben could certainly be proud of the part his leadership had played in such an accomplishment (*Küstner*)

the discrepancies sometimes encountered between pilots' own personal records and official sources.

After their frustrating failure to come to grips with the 20th Aero Squadron on the 16th, the pilots of *Jasta* 18 may have only rarely encountered American airmen again. The focus of the USAS turned north in anticipation of the Meuse-Argonne offensive, which would soon begin, and aerial operations in the St Mihiel area decreased considerably.

Like every other German aviation unit, *Staffel* Raben was no doubt hindered by the increasing scarcity of fuel and oil. Nonetheless, available records indicate that the unit achieved three confirmed victories against French fighters in 15 minutes on the afternoon of 21 September. Offz Stv Richard Schleichardt was credited with a SPAD over the Facq Woods at 1900 hrs for his third tally of the war. Five minutes later Hans Müller accounted for another SPAD in his usual fashion, this one falling near Pont à Mousson for his 12th and final confirmed victory of the war. At 1915 hrs Ltn d R Erich Spindler destroyed his second and final confirmed opponent, a SPAD that came down in the Combres Forest. It is impossible to match these victories and French losses with unquestionable validity.

A patrol from *Groupe de Combat* 16 was involved in a combat with 14 Fokker D VIIs over Cerney, and Sgt Frédéric Claudet of *Escadrille* SPA151 was shot down in flames – however, this combat is recorded as occurring at 0800 hrs (German and Allied time being the same at this period). *Jasta* 18's three victories were the only claims for SPADs made by German pilots this day, so perhaps someone made an error in timekeeping. Sgt Pierre Millot of SPA165 was wounded this day too, which may also relate to the *Jasta* Raben combats.

According to several sources, the next successful day for the pilots of *Jasta* 18 was 1 October. Although details of time and location are lacking, it is often reported that Heinz Küstner and Hans Muller were both credited with downing two more SPADs on this day. If accurate, this brought Müller's final total to 13 confirmed victories. As noted, though, his own accounting in the current possession of his family makes *no* mention of a claim on 1 October, and gives his total as 12 confirmed victories, with two *zur Landung gezwungen*.

Coincidentally, the first day of October saw yet two more losses suffered by the 13th Aero Squadron, Lts C A Brodie and G D Stivers both being killed in a fight with red-nosed Fokkers in the region of Andevanne-Bantheville. Other pilots of the 13th like Leighton Brewer believed that their friends fell to their old colourful opponents of 14 September. However, the two pilots died in a location quite distant from *Staffel* Raben's usual operating area. It is more likely they were shot down by three pilots from *Jasta* 15 – including Josef Veltjens – who claimed three SPADs destroyed southeast of Buzancy at 1640 hrs. Both the time and general location are good matches for the 13th Aero Squadron's losses.

It is entirely possible that records of a number of *Jasta* 18 victories in October and November have been lost or destroyed in the chaotic final days of the war. Certainly aerial combat continued, but only two more victories are known to this writer. On 10 October Kurt Monnington shot down a de Havilland in flames on the Allied side of the lines near Onville and Priester Woods for his seventh victory. It is possible this may have been an American DH 4 from the 8th Aero Squadron.

The final known *Luftsieg* for Monnington – and Royal Prussian *Jagdstaffel* 18 – was fittingly scored against the bombers of the IAF on 23 October. All three daylight squadrons of the IAF took off from Azelot that morning, headed for the triangle of railways at Metz-Sablon. As 12 DH 9s from No 104 Sqn neared their target they were shadowed by four Pfalz fighters.

This rare aerial view of the end of the hangar line at Montingen, taken shortly before the end of the war, shows three *Staffel* Raben Fokkers on the left and the unit's red and white DH 4 'hack' machine on the right in front of its own tent hangar. Note that two of the D VIIs have their tails painted in personal colours

After unleashing their payload, the bomber crews sighted more enemy scouts approaching from both their front and rear. The bomber formation was attacked from both directions by up to 15 hostile machines, and *Jasta* 18 was certainly in the mix of the opposition. Observer 2Lt White fired 250 rounds at a fighter with a red fuselage and 'blue and red striped undersurfaces on its lower wing' (most likely an impression of the printed camouflage or lozenge fabric).

The aggressive *Jagdflieger* positioned themselves between the two formations of DH 9s, diving to attack from the front then zooming back up to fire again from the rear. Kurt Monnington was credited with a DH 9 at 1315 hrs near Fourasse Wood. This was possibly aircraft D2932, with 2Lts Case (pilot) and Bridger both wounded and taken prisoner. However, one pilot from *Jasta* 64w and another from *KEST* 3 also successfully claimed DH 9s in this combat, although only one was actually shot down. One other de Havilland had to force-land on a French airfield after a lengthy pursuit by a German fighter. At any rate, Monnington had his eighth victory.

Perhaps the last time *Jasta* 18 was in action, albeit unsuccessfully, was on 3 November 1918. Capt Mackay of No 55 Sqn left on a reconnaissance flight toward Metz at 1030 hrs with observer 2Lt Gompertz. As they approached Metz in their DH 4, they sighted eight red and white D VIIs attempting to manoeuvre into favourable positions for an attack. Unfortunately for the *Jasta* Raben pilots, they failed to gain sufficient altitude and served merely as target practice for Gompertz. The observer fired 100 rounds at various Fokkers as they came near, and all of them spiralled away without attacking. The DH 4 crew returned unscathed.

With that disappointing encounter, the sparse record of *Jasta* 18 combats in the war's final months comes to an end. On 11 November 1918 the Armistice went into effect, and the disgruntled pilots of *Jasta* 18 had to accept the inevitable result. Two days later, they had a bitter pill to swallow – the men were ordered to fly their flamboyant, battle-scarred D VIIs to a collecting station at Saargemünd to be turned over to the Allies. With heavy hearts, the pilots of *Staffel* Raben landed their vermilion and white birds at the collection centre. As the Fokkers'

After the Armistice the Fokkers of *Staffel* Raben were flown to this collection depot at Saargemünd. Two *Jasta* 18 aircraft are seen at centre, one being a late-production D VII displaying Küstner's markings and the other resembling the machine photographed with Wilhelm Kühne much earlier. No doubt the proud pilots of *Jasta* Raben felt this was a sad end for their flamboyant machines

The familiar *Staffel* Raben D VII with a black chevron on the side shows up in a number of albums of American airmen

engines kicked over their last compressions, the pilots clambered out of their cockpits and reported to the commander of the station. Some probably took a final glance at the colourful machines that had carried them through so many fierce battles before heading off to demobilisation depots in Germany.

French and American airmen who encountered the interned D VIIs of *Jasta* 18 were intrigued by their dazzling colour schemes and markings. Some of the Fokkers were flown by their new owners, and photographs of these beautiful aircraft turn up in a number of albums of Allied pilots.

According to Heinz Küstner, *Jagdstaffel* 18 was credited with 126 confirmed victories during its two-year career. Historians have been unable to account for all of these. It is possible that some of the final victories were not confirmed or officially recorded due to the retreat and defeat of Germany's military forces. The late researcher Rick Duiven was able to come up with 112 confirmations (107 aeroplanes and five balloons), in exchange for the loss of eight pilots killed, eleven wounded and two taken prisoner. Whatever the actual record may have been, there is little doubt that the men who flew in the oft-changing roster of *Jasta* 18 composed a crack outfit. Under the excellent leadership of Grieffenhagen, Berthold and Raben, they were a force to be reckoned with, and were respected by friend and foe alike.

A *Jasta* 18 Fokker D VII, its guns removed, has its engine run up by its new American owners after the war. The wheel covers are from an OAW-built D VII, and the cowling panels seem to be a mix of OAW and Albatros parentage

APPENDICES

APPENDIX 1

JAGDSTAFFEL 18 COMMANDERS

Commander	Dates of Command	Notes
Oblt K H Grieffenhagen	31/10/16 to 24/4/17	WIA
Ltn von Bülow-Bothkamp	24/4/17 to 10/5/17	stv
Rittm K H Grieffenhagen	10/5/17 to 12/8/17	to JSch II
Oblt Rudolf Berthold	12/8/17 to 10/10/17	WIA
Oblt Ernst Wilhelm Turck	10/10/17 to 13/10/17	stv
Oblt Ernst Wilhelm Turck	13/10/17 to 5/3/18	
Hptm Rudolf Berthold	5/3/18 to 8/3/18	to command JGr 7
Oblt Hans-Joachim Buddecke	8/3/18 to 10/3/18	KIA
Oblt Ernst Wilhelm Turck	10/3/18 to 20/3/18	to *Jasta* 15
Ltn d R August Raben	20/3/18 to 20/3/18	injured in crash
Ltn Rodde	21/3/18 to 14/4/18	stv
Ltn d R August Raben	14/4/18 to 11/11/18	

Note

Those who were temporary acting commanders are noted as stv (stellvertreter)

APPENDIX 2

ACES WHO SERVED IN *JAGDSTAFFEL* 18

Name	Victories in *Jasta* 18	Overall victories
Hptm Rudolf Berthold	16	44
Ltn Hans Müller	10	12
Ltn Walter von Bülow-Bothkamp	9	28
Ltn d R Kurt Monnington	8	8
Ltn d R Richard Runge	7	8
Offz-Stv Wilhelm Kühne	7	7
Ltn d R Paul Strähle	7	14/15*
Ltn d R Ernst Wiessner	6	6
Oblt Harald Auffarth	5	26/31
Ltn d R Karl Albert Mendel	5	7
Ltn d R Josef Veltjens	5	34/35
Ltn Johannes Klein	2	16
Ltn Oliver von Beaulieu-Marconnay	0	25/26
Oblt Hans-Joachim Buddecke	0	13

Name	Victories in *Jasta* 18	Overall victories
Ltn Georg von Hantelmann	0	29
Oblt Otto Hartmann	0	7
Ltn Hans Viebig	0	5
Ltn d R Hugo Schäfer	0	12

Note

Two numbers in the overall victories column indicate, first, the total credited on most official lists and, second, the number cited by other sources or claimed by the pilot himself

APPENDIX 3

JASTA 18 PILOTS WHO RECEIVED THE *ORDEN POUR LE MERITE*

Recipient of award	Date of Award	Unit at Time of Award
Oblt Hans-Joachim Buddecke	14 April 1916	*Militär-Mission Türkei*
Hptm Rudolf Berthold	12 October 1916	*Jasta* 4
Ltn Walter von Bülow-Bothkamp	8 October 1917	*Jasta* 36
Ltn d R Josef Veltjens	16 August 1918	*Jasta* 15
Ltn Oliver von Beaulieu-Marconnay	26 October 1918	*Jasta* 19

APPENDIX 4

NOTES ON *JASTA* 18 AIRCRAFT

Aircraft	Pilot (if known)	Details
Albatros D III 1942/16	Ltn Flink	Captured 5 April 1917
Albatros D III 1978/16	Ltn d R Wiessner	Crashed spring 1917
Albatros D III 1954/16	Ltn von Bülow-Bothkamp	Spring/summer 1917, dark stripe
Albatros D III 1956/16	unknown	Spring/summer 1917
Albatros D III 2227/16	unknown	Marked similarly to 1954/16
FE 2d A5149	*Jasta* 'hack' and photo machine	Ex-No 20 Sqn, captured 7 May 1917
Albatros D III 1970/16	Ltn d R Strähle	August 1917
Albatros D III 1976/16	Ltn d R Strähle	August-September 1917
Albatros D V 1060/17	Ltn d Runge	Autumn 1917
Albatros D V 4594/17	Ltn d R Strähle	September 1917-January 1918, then to *Jasta* 57
Pfalz D III 4004/17	Oblt Berthold	October 1917
Albatros D Va 5253/17	Ltn d R Runge	KIA on 15 November 1917
Albatros D V 2171/17	Ltn von Beaulieu-Marconnay	January 1918
Albatros D Va 7387/17	Ltn d R Müller	5 May 1918 – 4th victory
Fokker D VII 386/18	Ltn d R Schultz	Captured 6 June 1918
Fokker D VII 2144/18	Vzfw Maürer	OAW-built, summer 1918
Fokker Dr I 479/17	Ltn d R Raben	May to November 1918
DH 4 A7703	*Jasta* 'hack' machine	Ex-No 55 Sqn, captured 30 August 1918

COLOUR PLATES

All of the art in this section was painstakingly created by Harry Dempsey, who patiently worked with the author to illustrate the aeroplanes and their colours as accurately as circumstances will permit. The colours portrayed are approximations based on the best available data. Many details are provisional, and are duly noted as such. The author owes a great debt to the research of such authorities as Alex Imrie, Manfred Thiemeyer, Michael Schmeelke, Ray Rimell, Dave Roberts, Dan-San Abbott and Bruno Schmäling.

1

Albatros D III 1954/16 of Ltn Walter von Bülow-Bothkamp, *Jasta* 18, Halluin, spring/summer 1917

It is believed that under Grieffenhagen's command during this early period, *Jasta* 18 aircraft generally featured only personal markings – often stripes or initials on the fuselage. This Albatros featured a basic factory finish typical of early production D IIIs. The fuselage plywood was 'natural varnished' and all metal cowling panels and struts were a dull greyish-green or grey. The uppersurfaces of the wings and tailplane/elevator were camouflaged in dark olive green, light Brunswick green and chestnut brown (Venetian Red) shades. The undersides of the wings and tailplane were light blue, and clear-doped linen covered the rudder, which displayed the Albatros factory logo. The only visible personal markings applied by von Bülow-Bothkamp consisted of a dark vertical stripe on the fuselage aft of the cockpit and dark wheel covers. This dark colour remains unconfirmed, but the author believes it may have been red. This is based, in part, on the cap band colour of von Bülow's hussar regiment.

2

Albatros D III (serial unknown) of Oblt Rudolf Berthold, *Jasta* 18, Harlebeke, September 1917

Once Berthold took over the *Staffel*, he had the aeroplanes of his command coloured in sympathy with the dress tunics of his pre-war army unit, *Infanterie-Regiment* Nr 20 'Graf Tauentzien'. The uppersurfaces of the fuselage and tail unit were uniformly painted a rather dark blue. This colour was sometimes (but not always) extended to the uppersurfaces of both wings, and this application has been tentatively depicted on Berthold's D III. The nose of each aircraft was painted red forward of the rear centre-section strut attachment. The underside of the fuselage was painted a light blue to match the undersurfaces of the wings and tailplane, thus providing a sort of 'sky camouflage'. This pale blue colour was usually extended to the undercarriage and wheel covers as well. Berthold personalised his mount with his famous white winged sword insignia, which he had first employed in *Jasta* 14. This emblem was applied to both sides of the fighter's fuselage and – uniquely – to the upper deck as well. Berthold was photographed with what was presumably this machine following his 25th victory, thus indicating that he was still flying the D III in September.

3

Albatros D V (serial unknown) of Ltn Otto Schober, *Jasta* 18, Harlebeke, September 1917

Ltn Schober flew at least two D Vs marked with a white five-pointed star as a personal emblem, although the stars were painted in differing attitudes on each. This one appears in the background of a photograph featuring Berthold's D III and a number of others at Halluin. The fighter displayed the usual colours of a dark blue fuselage with red nose. It is presumed that the uppersurfaces of both wings were also dark blue, but that is unconfirmed. This author believes that the centre-section struts of most of these aircraft were painted red, but that the interplane struts were more likely to have been painted dark blue. although he scored 'only' a single confirmed victory, Schober was a dependable and valued member of the Berthold *Staffel,* and his loss at the hands of Capt W G Barker on 26 October 1917 was keenly felt by his squadronmates.

4

Albatros D V (serial unknown) of Oblt Harald Auffarth, *Jasta* 18, Harlebeke, September 1917

Harald Auffarth was a rising star of *Jasta* 18 in September, quickly racking up his first five victories. His D V was marked with a beautifully delineated white comet emblem. Otherwise, this machine probably displayed standard *Staffel* colours and just possibly may have had dark blue uppersurfaces on both wings. When Auffarth's meteoric successes brought him command of *Jasta* 29 on 20 October, this D V was left behind for Oblt Turck (see *Osprey Aviation Elite Units 19 - Jagdgeschwader Nr II 'Geschwader 'Berthold'* for a photograph). Auffarth continued to use his comet emblem in *Jasta* 29, on Fokker D VII 287/18. He had achieved at least 26 victories (possibly as many as 31) by war's end, and was proposed for the *Pour le Mérite*, but this was not acted upon before the armistice.

5

Albatros D V (serial unknown) of Ltn d R Josef Veltjens, *Jasta* 18, Harlebeke, October 1918

Veltjens utilised his familiar white 'Indian Arrow' emblem on this well-photographed D V. This writer has previously believed that the uppersurfaces of the wings of Veltjens' Albatros were green/mauve camouflaged, but it is now considered that they were just as likely overpainted dark blue based on an examination of all available photographs. This machine otherwise displayed typical *Staffel* Berthold colours. Veltjens survived the war as commander of *Jasta* 15 in JG II, with at least 35 confirmed victories and the 'Blue Max'. In the immediate postwar period he served in the *Freikorps*, then sailed the North Sea in a yacht with his comrades Lohmann, Margot and von Ziegesar. After travelling the world as an arms dealer, Veltjens served in the Luftwaffe with the rank of oberst. Serving as Hermann Göring's personal emissary in Finland in 1940, he would perish three years later on 6 October 1943 on a flight to Rome in a Ju 52/3m provided by Feldmarschall Albert Kesselring. On Göring's behalf, Veltjens was to negotiate with Benito Mussolini for the removal of Italy's gold reserves to avoid capture by the approaching Allied forces. When the aeroplane landed in Milan, the pilot was informed that British fighters where out to intercept his flight. As the pilot attempted to cross the Appenine mountains, he flew as low as possible to evade the British aircraft, but the Ju 52/3m eventually crashed into the side of a mountain near Piacenza. With the exception of one crew member, all on board the transport were killed.

6

Albatros D V 4594/17 of Ltn d R Paul Strähle, *Jasta* 18, Harlebeke, November 1917

Strähle made his first flight in this D V on 5 October 1917, and would fly it in two different *Staffeln* on 130 flights. In addition to the usual blue and red colours on the fuselage, it is believed that the wings were covered in five-colour printed 'lozenge' camouflage fabric, but that the undersides were painted pale blue in common with other *Jasta* 18 aircraft. When writing to Harry van Dorssen in 1981, Strähle commented, 'I always had the undersides of the wings and fuselage of all my machines painted very light, probably light blue. In that way the machines were well camouflaged against the sky and hard to make out for flak gunners and enemy machines from below. The uppersurfaces of the wings were always left in the original "mimicry" colours [i.e., earth-imitation colours]'. Strähle's personal emblem was a white battle-axe. Close inspection of photographs reveals that some sort of non-standard covers were fitted over the machine gun ammunition chutes, and they are tentatively portrayed here. This machine was finally written off in a crash with *Jasta* 57 on 16 May 1918 after Strähle had flown it for over seven months.

7

Albatros D V (serial unknown) of Ltn Walter Dingel, Harlebeke, November 1917

Dingel is recorded as having employed a pale blue fuselage band as an individual emblem, and just such a marking appears in the photograph of him and his mechanics posing with this D V. It is assumed that the uppersurfaces of both wings were the same dark blue as the fuselage, but this is difficult to confirm. Dingel used a similar pale blue band on the Albatros D Va he later flew in *Jasta* 15, although the marking was somewhat wider on that machine. Dingel would later serve as technical officer of JG II under Berthold.

8

Albatros D III (OAW, serial unknown) of Oblt Ernst Wilhelm Turck, Harlebeke, October/November 1917

Turck employed at least two variations of a personal marking of vertical black and white bands on his D III fighters. The insignia as seen on this OAW-built D III displayed these colours in the proportions of the ribbon for the Iron Cross medal. It is assumed that the wings were dark blue on top and light blue underneath, but this remains difficult to prove. Note the modifications in the form of additional cooling louvres cut into the scout's metal cowling panels, also seen on at least one other *Jasta* 18 D III.

9

Pfalz D III 4004/17 of Oblt Rudolf Berthold, *Jasta* 18, Harlebeke, October 1917

It would appear that Berthold acquired this Pfalz D III sometime in late September or early October 1917. He probably did not fly it for very long before he was wounded on 10 October. At any rate, there was time to have the machine carefully painted in the red and dark blue *Staffel* colours, and for another version of Berthold's white winged sword emblem to be applied. The military serial number was still visible through the blue paint on the interplane strut and aft fuselage, as was the fuselage cross. The Pfalz's undercarriage and wheel covers retained their factory finish, while the fuselage and wing undersides were probably painted in this silver-grey colour as well.

10

Pfalz D III (serial unknown) of Ltn Hans Burckhard von Buttlar, *Jasta* 18, Avelin, January 1918

Buttlar described this aircraft as his first assigned *Jagdeinsitzer* at *Jasta* 18. It apparently bore standard unit colours in all locations, including dark blue uppersurfaces on the wings. The personal badge was a white man-in-the-moon (with pipe) insignia on both sides of the fuselage. Precise details of this emblem are difficult to discern, and the interpretation illustrated is based on the enhancement of the sole available photograph and the artist's best judgement.

11

Albatros D V 2171/17 of Ltn Oliver *Freiherr* von Beaulieu-Marconnay, *Jasta* 18, Avelin, January 1918

A relative latecomer to the Berthold *Staffel,* von Beaulieu-Marconnay wasted little time in applying his own embellishments to his D V. It sported the usual dark blue on the fuselage, tail and wing uppersurfaces, as well as the unit's red nose. The pilot's personal emblem was inspired by the branding iron insignia of his cavalry unit, *Dragoner-Regiment* Nr 4 *'von Bredow'*. The aircraft's military serial number D 2171/17 on the fin is still just visible through the dark blue paint on the original print of the photograph. The same pilot apparently later flew a similar D V or D Va in *Jasta* 15, but on that machine the wings retained their original green/mauve camouflage.

12

Pfalz D III (pilot and serial unknown), *Jasta* 18, Avelin, winter 1917-18

Unfortunately, the pilot of this beautiful Pfalz remains unidentified, but there is a slight possibility he may have been Ltn Kleffel. The machine displayed complete *Staffel* livery, with both wings painted dark blue on top. The personal emblem consisted of three white intertwined rings on the fuselage. Ace Friedrich Altemeier of *Jasta* 24 employed a similar insignia, his being based on the logo of the Krupp Factory where he had once worked. However, the origin of this unknown *Jasta* 18 pilot's symbol is a mystery.

13

Albatros D V (pilot and serial unknown), *Jasta* 18, Avelin, December 1917

Unfortunately, details concerning this aircraft – including the approximate date and location of the photographs that were taken of it – are lacking. The pilot may have been a believer in lucky charms, as his personal markings consisted of a four-leaf clover inside a horseshoe. The crash photograph of this aeroplane reveals that the uppersurface of the top wing, at least, was left in factory finish of green and mauve camouflage. At the time of the crash, the port horizontal stabiliser was covered in five-colour printed camouflage fabric.

14

Pfalz D IIIa (serial unknown) of Gefr Max Hitschler, Jasta 18, Avelin, January 1918

Hitschler's Pfalz bore Jasta 18 livery on all surfaces, with the undersides of the wings, tail and fuselage retaining their original silver-grey finish. The individual insignia was made up of five white vertical stripes, which seem to have been confined to the dark blue display on the upper fuselage and did not extend to the underside. When Hitschler left for Jasta 57 at the end of January, this machine was taken over by von Buttlar, who had the rings painted over. He then added his own emblem of a hunting horn, inspired by the helmet crest on his family's coat of arms. In common with some other Pfalz machines of the Jasta, this D IIIa had its spinner removed.

15

Albatros D Va (pilot and serial unknown), Jasta 18, Lomme, May 1918

Illustrating the early form of Staffel Raben unit markings, this profile is provisionally based on a very small image in a line-up photograph. The nose was vermilion red from the cockpit forward, with a white spinner, and the rest of the fuselage and tail was white. The tailplane and elevators displayed broad diagonal black and white chevron markings as part of the pilot's personal identification. The black stripe on the fuselage was an additional individual emblem. The uppersurface of the top wing may have been red, with large white panels for the early Balkenkreuz insignia. This D Va, possibly OAW-built, has previously been depicted with a 'lozenge' fabric lower wing. However, close inspection of the (admittedly poor) photograph seems to indicate a green/mauve camouflage pattern on the bottom wing as depicted here.

16

Albatros D Va (pilot and serial unknown), Jasta 18, Lomme, May 1918

Another early D Va in Staffel Raben livery, this aircraft probably had a red uppersurface on the top wing, with the lower wing retaining its five-colour camouflage printed fabric finish. Again, the crosses on the upper wing were displayed against large white panels. The black three-pointed 'Mercedes Star' was also seen on later D VII machines flown by Heinz Küstner. It is unlikely Küstner flew this D Va, however, for when he arrived on 7 July 1918 the unit was probably equipped entirely with the Fokker D VII. Thus, Küstner may have inherited the star emblem from some other pilot.

17

Albatros D Va (serial unknown) of Ltn Kurt Monnington, Jasta 18, Lomme, May 1918

Monnington had earlier employed a more detailed version of a death's head insignia on his Jasta 15 D V, and chose to use a black silhouette version on this D Va. There was a wide range of Balkenkreuz insignia formats and sizes seen on these Staffel Raben D Va Albatros fighters. The depiction of the red upper wing finish here is strictly provisional.

18

Pfalz D IIIa (serial unknown) of Ltn d R Hans Müller(?), Jasta 18, Lomme, April 1918

This depiction is largely provisional, being based on the partial photograph of Müller posing by the nose of a heavily damaged Pfalz D IIIa. This aircraft clearly had the usual Staffel Raben colours, including the raven emblem, in the typical locations. It is not possible to determine if the machine displayed Müller's usual personal emblems of a diagonally striped fuselage band and chevron-striped tailplane (see his D VII in Profile 26) from the limited view of the damaged aircraft. However, a rather indistinct photograph of the Albatros D Va with the 'Mercedes Star' emblem (Profile 16) also shows a Pfalz D IIIa in the background with nothing more than the raven emblem on its white fuselage. This profile, then, provisionally depicts that machine. Perhaps at the time it was the unit's sole Pfalz D IIIa, and there was no need for further personal emblems.

19

Albatros D Va (pilot and serial unknown), Jasta 18, Lomme, June 1918

When he flew in Jasta 39 in Italy Ltn d R Raben employed a version of a raven emblem, which differed somewhat from the familiar one seen on the red and white machines of Jasta 18. This enigmatic D Va first appears in the line-up photograph taken at Lomme with a small black bird emblem on its fin, which resembles that early raven emblem utilised by Raben. A later photograph indicates that the emblem was painted over with opaque white, or else removed. This aircraft may have once been flown by Raben, but that is certainly unconfirmed. This D Va also displayed a personal marking of black/white stripes on the fuselage.

20

Fokker D VII 386/18 of Ltn d R Hans Schultz, Jasta 18, Lomme, June 1918

Schultz was captured on 6 June, and there are two technical reports concerning his Fokker D VII. Sadly, no photographs of the aircraft with its fabric intact are known, but this illustration is provisionally based on the description in the reports and on an artist's sketch made before the fabric was stripped. 386/18 was an early Fokker-built D VII, and the fuselage left the factory in streaky olive-green camouflage before it was painted vermilion and white. In the past, the military serial number of this aircraft has been incorrectly reported as either 1450 or 2455. In actuality, those numbers are respectively the factory wing number and the works number of this machine. The uppersurfaces of both wings of 386/18 were vermilion, but the undersides remained in five-colour printed fabric. The aforementioned sketch depicts two vertical black stripes on the fuselage, but pointedly does not show any raven emblem, so it is not portrayed here. The white decoration of the spinner seen on the Jasta's previous Albatros and Pfalz machines was transferred to the radiator shell of the Fokker D VIIs.

21

Fokker D VII (Alb) flown by Ltn d R Heinz Küstner, Jasta 18, Montingen, August 1918

Küstner's well-photographed Albatros-built D VII featured

the black 'Mercedes Star' mentioned earlier, and displayed striking reverse chevron-style stripes in black and white(?) on the tailplane and elevators. Although some *Staffel* Raben D VIIs may have had the vermilion colouring extended to the wing undersurfaces, it is evident from photographs that several certainly did not. The D VIIs profiled here are provisionally depicted as having printed 'lozenge' fabric undersides, but some may eventually have had those surfaces painted red. In common with other Fokker D VIIs of the unit, Küstner's machine was equipped with a flare pistol mounted on the top wing centre section, a rack for cartridges beside the cockpit and had additional cooling holes cut into the engine cowling.

22

Fokker D VII (Alb) of Ltn d R August Raben, *Jasta* 18, Montingen, August 1918

Tentatively described as an Albatros-built D VII, this Fokker has been considered an OAW product by some. The aircraft of the *Staffelführer* was unique in having the vermilion display extended to the leading edge of the tailplane, and in featuring the raven insignia in white. This certainly made the scout easy to identify in the air, and as Alex Imrie has pointed out, 'Although the difference in colour was sufficient for identification, there was another connotation in that a *"weisser Rabe"* was a rare bird indeed!' Raben was a respected leader who suffered five wartime wounds, but apparently two of them were slight and he was only awarded a Wound Badge in silver. In 1919 he took part the Russian Civil War, serving on the staff of the *Kommandeur der Flieger* of the Russian West Army formed to fight the communists. Raben was subsequently awarded the German-Russian West Army Volunteer Awaloff (Avalov) Cross following his service in this conflict.

23

Fokker D VII (OAW) of Ltn d R Kurt Monnington, *Jasta* 18, Montingen, August 1918

Certain features visible on close inspection of the photograph indicate that Kurt Monnington's D VII was probably an early OAW product. This machine was emblazoned with Monnington's usual death's head insignia as well as black borders on all aft fuselage and tail surfaces. The latter added an even more sinister aspect to this D VII. Among German airmen, white aircraft that boasted black linings were sometimes called 'flying death announcements' for their similarity to black-outlined obituary notices! Monnington's D VII featured an anemometer-type ASI affixed to the starboard interplane strut.

24

Fokker D VII (OAW) (serial and pilot unknown), *Jasta* 18, Montingen, August 1918

The unidentified pilot of this OAW-built D VII chose to personalise his mount with coloured chordwise stripes on the tailplane/elevators and borders of the same colour applied to the fuselage, fin and rudder. This colour is unknown, but green is a logical possibility. Like many other *Jasta* 18 D VIIs, this machine was modified through the addition of a signal pistol and flare cartridge rack. Note the cooling holes cut into the engine cowling. Added in the field by *Jasta* mechanics, these could vary slightly from one machine to the next. Like Monnington's D VII featured

above, this aircraft also has an anemometer-type ASI affixed to its starboard interplane strut

25

Fokker D VII (Alb) (serial unknown) of Ltn d R Günther von Büren, Montingen, September 1918

Günther von Büren chose to add four plump chicks running beneath the raven emblem as his personal identification. The similarity of these chick markings suggests that they were applied with a stencil, just as the *Staffel* insignia was. Ltn d R von Büren also fitted his D VII with an Oigee telescopic sight, as well as the usual *Jasta* 18 accessories. This pilot attained two confirmed victories before being wounded in the one-sided encounter with the SPAD XIIIs of the 13th Aero Squadron on 14 September 1918.

26

Fokker D VII (Alb) (serial unknown) of Ltn d R Hans Müller, *Jasta* 18, Montingen, September 1918

This profile is based on the previously unpublished photograph of Müller's Albatros-built D VII provided by historian Jörn Leckscheid. Müller had consistently marked his fighters in *Jastas* 15 and 18 with the black and white diagonally striped fuselage band as seen on this D VII. He also usually added stripes to the tailplane and elevators in a similar motif. Otherwise, this D VII bore the unit's flamboyant colours in typical style. It had a rear-view mirror affixed to the top wing centre section and the usual rack for flare cartridges on the starboard side of the cockpit.

27

Fokker Dr I 479/17 of Ltn d R August Raben, *Jasta* 18, Montingen, October 1918

According to Heinz Küstner and evidence from photographs, there was only one triplane on the strength of *Staffel* Raben, and it was the mount of the *Staffelführer*. When photographed at Lomme in May, this machine bore large white cross fields on the top wing and the white raven emblem had not yet been applied. It was later photographed in French hands after the war, and this illustration is based on those images. The previous white panels on the top wing were discernible through the red overpaint, and by the post-war period the white paint on the fuselage and rudder was considerably degraded. One of the photographs indicates that the interplane struts were probably not red as widely supposed, but were more likely factory finish light undersurface blue. It is also possible that the undersides of the wings were red by this date, but we have conservatively chosen to depict them as factory finish. The cowling was white, and wheel covers may have been a worn and dirtied red. Alex Imrie has reported the serial number of this Dr I as 479/17.

28

DH 4 A7703, *Staffel* 'hack' machine, *Jasta* 18, October 1918

This DH 4 was an ex-No 55 Sqn aircraft that had been forced down on 30 August 1918 during a raid on the Thionville railway sidings, most likely by Ltn d R Raben. The crew of 2Lt H H Doehler (an American) and 2Lt A S Papworth were both taken prisoner. After being transported to the airfield at Montingen, the DH 4 was painted on all uppersurfaces in the *Staffel* colours of vermilion and white, even including the white radiator marking. Late war *Balkenkreuz* insignia were applied to the white rudder and upper and lower wing surfaces. It is the author's belief that the undersurfaces of the wings and tailplane retained their clear-doped fabric finish. From available photographs it does not seem that the *Jasta* insignia of a black raven was marked on the aircraft – at least when the available photos were taken.

ACKNOWLEDGEMENTS

The author owes a very great debt to Australian historian Russ Gannon, who generously made his years of research into matching *Jasta* claims and losses with British records available for this work. In most cases, when a *Jasta* victory over a British aircraft is identified or a casualty is attributed to an Allied airman in this volume, it is based on Russ' *Jasta* 18 compilation. As always, grateful thanks goes to Dieter H M Gröschel, MD, for sharing valuable information from his studies and reviewing the text. The assistance and research of Alex Imrie, Manfred Thiemeyer, Michael Schmeelke, Bruno Schmäling and Thomas Genth is greatly appreciated. Adam Wait and O'Brien Browne provided indispensable translations of German material, and this book would not have been possible without them. Thanks are extended to Lance Bronnenkant, Reinhard Kastner, Jörn Leckscheid, Thomas Genth and Reinhard Zankl for use of their valuable photographs. Stefan Bruhns provided indispensable access to the photographs of *Jasta* 18 mechanic Johann Rief. The author's gratitude is extended to Tony Holmes and Harry Dempsey for their infinite patience, gracious goodwill and superb contributions to this book. The staff members of the History of Aviation Collection in the University of Texas at Dallas were helpful as always. Dan-San Abbott, Jim Miller, Robert Karr, Immo Frese, Peter Kilduff, Jon Guttman, Ray Rimell, Dave Roberts and too many others to name all gave unselfishly of their time and material. The author would be remiss if he failed to acknowledge the contribution of his late colleagues Rick Duiven, Harry Van Dorssen (who transcribed the Strähle diaries) and A E Ferko (his superb book on *Jasta* 18 inspired the present work). The author's many colleagues at *Over the Front* (www.overthefront.com), *Cross and Cockade International* (www.crossandcockade.com), and the *Aerodrome Forum* (www.theaerodrome.com) were helpful as always.

BIBLIOGRAPHY

BARKER, W G, 'My Most Thrilling Sky Fight', *Sky Fighters*, Vol XIII No 3, June 1936

BIDDLE, C J, *The Way of the Eagle*, New York, 1919

BREWER, L, 'How It Was in the 13th Aero Squadron', *Cross & Cockade Journal*, Vol 3 No 1, Spring 1962

BREWER, L, *Riders in the Sky*, Boston, 1934

BRONNENKANT, L, PH D, *The Imperial German Eagles in World War I*, Volume 1 and Volume 2, Atglen, PA, 2006 and 2008

CROSS & COCKADE INTERNATIONAL, *FE 2b/d & Variants in RFC, RAF & AFC Service*, London, 2009

CROSS & COCKADE INTERNATIONAL, *Nieuports in RNAS, RFC and RAF Service*, London, 2007

FEDDERS, P, 'The German-American Air War at St Mihiel and Meuse-Argonne in Late 1918', *Over the Front*, Vol 24, No 1, Spring 2009

FERKO, A E, *Fliegertruppe 1914-1918 Nr 2, Staffel Raben 1918*, Salem, 1896

FRANKS, N, BAILEY, F, AND GUEST, R, *Above the Lines*, London, 1993

FRANKS, N, GUEST, G, AND BAILEY, F, *Bloody April . . . Black September*, London 1995

FRANKS, N, BAILEY, F AND DUIVEN, R, *The Jasta Pilots*, London, 1996

FRANKS, N, BAILEY, F AND DUIVEN, R, *The Jasta War Chronology*, London, 1998

GENGLER, L F, *Rudolf Berthold*, Berlin, 1934

GROSZ, P M, 'The Agile and Aggressive Albatros', *Air Enthusiast No 1*, 1976

GROSZ, P M, *Albatros D III*, Windsock Datafile Special, Berkhamsted, 2003

GUTTMAN, J, 'Paul Frank Baer – The Star-Spangled Ace', *Windsock International*, Vol 5 No 1 Spring 1989

GUTTMAN, J, *Osprey Aircraft of the Aces 88 - Pusher Aces of World War 1*, Botley, Oxford, 2009

GUTTMAN, J, *Osprey Aviation Elite Units 17 - SPA124 Lafayette Escadrille*, Botley, Oxford, 2004

GUTTMAN, J, *Osprey Duel 17 - SPAD XIII vs Fokker D VII, Western Front 1918*, Botley, Oxford, 2009

HARTNEY, H E, *Up and At' Em*, Harrisburg, PA, 1940

HENSHAW, T, *The Sky Their Battlefield*, London 1995

HOLT, W S, *The Great War at Home and Abroad*, Manhattan, KS, 1999

IMRIE, A, *Osprey Airwar 13 - German Fighter Units 1914-May 1917*, London, 1978

IMRIE, A, *Osprey Airwar 17 - German Fighter Units June 1917-1918*, London, 1978

IMRIE, A, *Pictorial History of the German Army Air Service*, London, 1971

IMRIE, A, *The Fokker Triplane*, London, 1992

IMRIE, A, *Vintage Warbirds 16 - German Army Air Aces of World War One*, Poole, 1987

O'CONNOR, N, *Aviation Awards of Imperial Germany in*

World War I and the Men Who Earned Them, Vols I to VII, Princeton NJ and Atglen PA, 1988 to 2003

PUGLISI, W R, ED./TRANSLATORS, 'Portrait of a Pilot – Paul Strähle, *Jasta 57, A War Diary from 3 May 1918 to 11 November 1918', Cross & Cockade Journal,* Vol 12 No 3, Autumn 1971

RALPH, W, *Barker VC,* London 1997

RENNLES, KEITH, *Independent Force, The War Diary of the Daylight Squadrons of the Independent Air Force June-November 1918,* London 2002

REVELL, A, *British Single-Seater Fighter Squadrons on the Western Front in World War I,* Atglen, PA, 2006

REVELL, A, *High in the Empty Blue,* Mountain View, 1995

REVELL, A, *Osprey Aviation Elite Units 33 - No 56 Sqn RAF/RFC,* Botley, Oxford, 2009

RIMELL, R, *Albatros Fighters Special,* Berkhamsted, 1991

RIMELL, R, 'The Ravens of *Jasta 18', Windsock International,* Vol 10, No 2, March/April 1994

RIMELL, R (ED), *Fokker D VII Anthology Nos 1, 2* and *3,* Berkhamsted, 1997, 2000 and 2002

SAPRU, SOMNATH, 'Flying Sikh – Hardit Singh Malik', *Cross & Cockade Great Britain Journal,* Vol 6 No 4, 1975

SCHMEELKE, M, 'Die Königliche Preussische *Jagdstaffel* 18', *Propellerblatt,* Nummer 6, Früjahr, 2003

STURTIVANT, R AND PAGE, G, *The DH 4/DH 9 File,* Turnbridge Wells, Kent, 1999

VANWYNGARDEN, G, *Osprey Aircraft of the Aces 77 - Albatros Aces of World War 1, Part 2,* Botley, Oxford, 2007

VANWYNGARDEN, G, *Osprey Aviation Elite Units 19 - Jagdgeschwader Nr II, Geschwader 'Berthold',* Botley, Oxford, 2005

VELTJENS, K, *Seppl – A Step Ahead of Politics,* createspace.com, 2009

VON DORSSEN, HARRY, ED., D G TUBBS AND W EVANS, TRANSLATORS, 'Paul Strähle, The War Diary of a German Aviator 11 August 1917 to 22 April 1918', *Cross & Cockade Great Britain Journal,* Vol 11 No 4, Winter 1980

ZUERL, W, *Pour le Mérite-Flieger,* Munich, 1938

www.buddecke.de

www.flieger-album.de

www.frontflieger.de

www.theaerodrome.com

INDEX

References to illustrations are shown in **bold**. Colour plates have captions on the page in brackets.

127